BECOMING
THE COMPLETE
ADULT

BECOMING THE COMPLETE ADULT

edited by

SIMON DONIGER

ASSOCIATION PRESS   New York

Becoming the Complete Adult

Copyright © 1962 by

National Board of Young Men's Christian Associations

Association Press, 291 Broadway, New York 7, N.Y.

Publisher's title stock number: 1496

Library of Congress catalog card number: 62-16868

 72

Printed in the United States of America

To Ann

CONTENTS

Becoming the Complete Adult

A LOOK AT WHAT IT MEANS . . .

Becoming the Complete Adult
Introduction

A LOOK
AT WHAT
IT MEANS

by Simon Doniger, author, Editor of *Pastoral Psychology,* and Fellow of the American Ortho-psychiatric Association

*"Gnothi seauton" (know yourself) has been
seen as the goal of all human endeavor ... but
it cannot be the goal if it is not at the same
time the beginning. The ethical individual knows
himself, but this knowledge is not a mere con-
templation ... it is a reflection upon himself
which itself is an action, and therefore I have
deliberately preferred to use the expression
"choose oneself" instead of "know oneself" ...
when the individual knows himself and has
chosen himself he is about to realize himself.—*
Søren Kierkegaard

In a very real sense, this statement by Kierkegaard expresses
the basic purpose and intent of this book—because maturity
involves self-acceptance, "choosing oneself," as well as an acceptance of the demands which the world makes upon each one
of us individually. Becoming an adult means accepting and then
transcending our personal needs, so that we see life in terms of
larger, more ultimate values.

Gaining self-knowledge is the first step toward maturity.
Intellectual knowledge alone, as we have so sadly discovered, is
not enough; for unless it is somehow harnessed to the emotional
life of a person, to his feelings, knowledge remains sterile. Man
is both thought and feeling, and the two cannot be separated if
he is to achieve a unity, a wholeness, a self-realization and self-
completion. As Carl Gustav Jung says, "If one or the other
aspect is lacking to him, the result is injury or at least a lopsided-
ness that may easily veer towards the pathological. Too much of
the animal distorts the civilized man, too much civilization makes
sick animals."

11

Our concern in this book is to provide young adult readers with some of the basic essentials for understanding and integrating these two aspects of themselves. Ten well-known authorities, speaking out of rich practical experience, discuss vital questions that we all need to ask ourselves—and try to answer—in the process of growing into full adulthood.

Dr. Dana L. Farnsworth talks about "Understanding Your Body," its functions and malfunctions, including growth during the various stages of life and the anxieties and worries which frequently accompany this growth. He discusses the relationship of the body to one's whole self, and takes a frank look at such matters as smoking and the use of alcohol and drugs. Helpfully included in his chapter are descriptions of symptoms of various illnesses, including venereal diseases, skin disorders, glandular disturbances, mononucleosis, and epilepsy.

The chapter on "Your Basic Psychology," by Dr. O. Spurgeon English and Dr. Francis H. Hoffman, traces some of the inevitable frustrations that accompany the growth of a child and development into adolescence, and indicate how our handling of these frustrations will affect future character and personality. The light of dynamic psychology and psychoanalysis is brought to bear upon the early personal growth stages that are already passed and the adjusting and maturing experiences that are yet to be encountered.

In the chapter on "Religious and Spiritual Values," Dr. Paul W. Pruyser and Dr. Karl A. Menninger show what values are, and why, without a system of values, our instinctual urges would lead to chaos and self-destruction. Here, however, we must distinguish between kinds of values: there are the values of a Nero or Eichmann, on the one hand, and those of a Lincoln or Schweitzer on the other. Then what kind of values are needed if an individual is to "choose himself," as Kierkegaard would say, and move on into a genuine concern and love for others? Perhaps the most important contribution in the chapter is this: If values are "those directive ideas on the basis of which one is willing to make great sacrifices," then we need to be sure that our values are genuinely constructive and freely chosen, and are not just compulsive or pathological reactions to the unavoidable frustrations of growing up.

"Becoming an Adult Sexually," by Dr. Ralph G. Eckert, is a discussion of the basic elements of sex and love: sex feelings, masturbation, petting, dating, going steady, early marriages, the difference in sex attitudes between men and women, and the role that sex plays in making a marriage complete. The author also speaks about parental difficulties, the effects of rejection, and the pathological substitutes for which sex is often used. Especially valuable is the description of those attitudes which will enable a young couple to grow into emotional maturity together and make the most out of marriage.

Dr. Harold Taylor, in "The Meaning of Education," asks some pertinent and provocative questions: Is education merely an acquisition of knowledge and facts, or is it primarily a preparation for a way of life? Should and can college education be separated from life, or should we find ways of integrating it with practical living and working? The author has been in the forefront of the battle for the kind of education that goes beyond the mere acquisition of information, and any reader—whether in college or out of college—will gain from this chapter a significant understanding both of education and of the ways in which he personally can achieve the kind of education that can be most meaningful to him.

Deciding upon one's vocation is an exciting, and *serious,* undertaking. A hit-and-miss, trial-and-error approach, as Dr. Elliott Dunlap Smith tells us in "Choosing a Vocation," can lead to a life of enervating drudgery instead of stimulating the growth and confidence that are the rewards of a well-chosen vocation. Dr. Smith gives the various practical criteria which help an individual to see what vocations are most closely related to his skills, interests, and personality. He shows what to look for in investigating vocations and how to narrow down the list of possibilities to make a final choice. There are two excellent step-by-step "Plans," which bring the question of vocation into its full perspective by considering the individual, the vocation itself, and the significance of a particular vocation in the modern world.

In "The Young Citizen in a World like This," Drs. Harry A. and Bonaro Overstreet discuss some of the broader aspects of living as they confront the younger generation. The chapter includes a thoughtful discussion of the psychologically healthy citizen, the democratic process, the problem of our "bigness," the loss of intimacy in government as well as in individual living, the problem of conformity and dissent, the various "isms," and the choices which might be made as a result of understanding these isms. They cite the relative value of diversity in unity, of competition, the contribution of the social services to our civilization, the danger of alienation and apathy on the part of any individual, and the great need for personal involvement not only with one's community but—as a citizen of the world—with the totality of mankind.

It was not intended by the editor, and surely it was not intended by the authors, that theirs should be the final word in these vital areas. As a matter of fact, we are sure that there are many things in these chapters with which some of our readers may and will disagree—such things as the psychoanalytic orientation of Dr. English and Dr. Hoffman, or the "moralism" of Dr. Eckert, or the "progressiveness" of Dr. Taylor, or what may seem to some readers the rather arbitrary attitude of the Overstreets toward ideologies other than our own—and this is as it should be. Their chapters are but a base from which to begin the search for an understanding of one's self, one's experiences and ideas, one's needs and desires, one's existential "predicament" and hope of self-fulfillment. "Modern man," writes Dr. Frederick A. Weiss in *The American Journal of Psychoanalysis,* "becomes more and more alienated from his self and his fellow men, from his nature and his culture, from his work and his leisure, from his body and his sex, from his feelings and from his creative potential. This all-pervasive alienation has become a main phenomenon of our culture." And yet in spite of, or possibly as a result of, this alienation, there is a constant search going on among young adults today for a sense of identity, for a deeper self-understanding, for answers to the questions "Who am I, and what am I, and where am I going?"

To provide a complete answer to such questions, and to that search, one might have included in this book a number of things which of necessity have been omitted. We might have included, for instance, material from the new science of anthropology on the contribution which our study of alien cultures has made and can make to our understanding of ourselves. It would have been valuable to include a chapter on how literature, music, painting, and sculpture affect our emotional development. The new leisure coming with the constant reduction in the work day is certainly something which is deeply relevant to our self-understanding and self-fulfillment. Will such leisure contribute to greater maturity and creativeness, or will it convert our population into passive TV watchers and time wasters? A discussion of our economy, including business and business ethics, industry, advertising, and labor unions, would have been valuable. And unquestionably, a book such as this might have had in it a discussion of the great world problems which face us today: disarmament, the cold war, the testing of atomic weapons, the "population explosion," the role of science and technology in modern life, and the potential of these for beneficial as well as destructive effects.

These are all areas of tremendous importance. But our purpose here has been to approach the more immediate problems first, those related to an individual's feelings and ideas about himself, so that he can "choose himself" and then move in the direction of transcending his own interests and becoming maturely involved in the world around him. "Human beings who are torn and distracted by internal insecurities and anxieties," says Professor Ashley Montagu, the noted anthropologist, in *Education and Human Relations,* "cannot long endure. A people made up of such persons must eventually founder on the rock of its own false values. External defenses can never make up for the lack of internal controls. What we need to do is to build internal controls in human beings, so that they can withstand external pressures and maintain internal equilibrium."

It is the attainment of this "internal equilibrium" that is the goal of this book; it is our hope that the self-knowledge gained through reading these chapters will help the reader to achieve the kind of self-realization that Kierkegaard talks about, both in relation to his own life and in relation to his fellow men.

Becoming the Complete Adult
Physically

UNDERSTANDING
YOUR
BODY

by Dana L. Farnsworth, M.D., Henry K. Oliver
Professor of Hygiene and Director of University Health Services, Harvard University

1

MAINTAINING health may be expensive in time, care, and occasionally money, but a continuing state of good health is very convenient and rewarding. Illness is even more expensive and is, in addition, frustrating and a source of fear or anxiety. In schools and colleges which have good health services, each student consults a physician on the average of about five or six times yearly. Some of these visits involve illness or injury, some the prevention of disability, and others the promotion of health. Proper health maintenance requires that you know enough about yourself to co-operate intelligently with the health agencies in your community.

The advances made by science and technology in raising material standards of living have also enormously benefited both personal and public health. In fact, a major source of concern about the future of the human race, the explosive increase in population in nearly all parts of the world, has been attributed in part to improvements in medical science which enable infants and young people to avoid or survive many formerly fatal diseases. The upper limits of life expectancy are no greater than a century ago, but many more persons can now be expected to live out their full span of life. Thus the percentage of people over 65 is rising steadily. Their health is of concern not only to them but to younger people as well, because of costs of medical care and changes in family structure brought about by the crowded conditions of urban and suburban living.

Health has many components involving education, economics, government, science, and almost every aspect of human activity. Since most people still think of health as a matter of luck, the full force of social pressures has not yet been brought to bear on the basic problem of health maintenance. As the complexities of health and disease become more clearly understood, demands for appropriate action increase. In the United States, the National Institutes of Health have been established out of the concern of the people about this problem. This government agency is making enormous efforts to co-ordinate presently available knowledge that will promote health and to advance that knowledge through research on all kinds of physical and mental diseases.

Public and private agencies working on health promotion would be more effective if the individuals about whom they are concerned knew more about themselves and how to co-operate with physicians and other health workers in protecting their health. Health educators have always had an uphill battle in their efforts to impart information which they know will be extremely valuable to all young people. A former director of health at Smith College once remarked that a girl is not interested in well-fitting shoes until her feet hurt. At no time is a person so ready and eager to learn as when something causes him pain or uneasiness.

GENERAL HEALTH QUESTIONS

During the turbulent years of adolescence many health questions arise in young people's minds because of variations in rate of growth and development. Sensitivity regarding all kinds of physical states is usual during these years. It is wise to remember that there is no set pattern which every "normal" person must follow. Very rapid growth is usual in boys between 12 and 16 and in girls a year or so earlier, but some people continue to grow considerably even after those ages. Furthermore, growth in different parts of the body may occur unevenly, giving rise to considerable awkwardness. The development of sexual organs and secondary sexual characteristics may cause much anxiety if not understood properly. For example, prominence of the breasts in young boys (gynecomastia) is very common for a few months during adolescence. Many fears center around the size of genital organs and the amount and distribution of pubic and axillary hair. An undescended testis is a serious problem to any adolescent boy or young man, partly because of the physical complications and otherwise because of the emotional aspects of the situation. Some boys who have this condition receive care for it before adolescence. Others are not treated for a variety of reasons. Many boys are very sensitive about this condition and find that otherwise ordinary situations may make them uncomfortable. Taking showers with other boys may be a source of embarrassment, since they may feel that in some way this condition reflects on their manliness. A person with this condition should get the best surgical opinion he can as soon as practicable and in the meantime avoid strenuous contact sports such as football, hockey, or soccer.

For girls the onset of menstrual periods may be a source of much concern, especially if it is delayed for a year or two in comparison with the experience of their friends. Likewise, the rate and extent of breast development is often the focus of much worry. There is no substitute for a good examination by a wise physician, with appropriate reassurance or adequate treatment if abnormalities are present.

Some young people are troubled greatly by acne; others have none. The amount of misinformation about acne which is current in the gossip circles of most communities is very great indeed. Actually it is the result of an endocrine imbalance typical of the period of rapid adjustment and change and has nothing to do with masturbation or any other sex habits. Its severity may vary depending upon heredity, cleanliness, oiliness of skin, emotional conflicts, insufficient rest and sleep, and other similar factors. The treatment of acne, therefore, should take into consideration all the factors in an individual's life which encourage or inhibit good health.

A good principle which should be followed by everyone is to find a physician in whom one can have confidence and go to him for information and advice whenever any health questions arise which provoke fear or anxiety. Parents can help by aiding their adolescent children in finding a physician who will be interested in their problems—the young person should feel that the physician is interested in his own special situations rather than feeling classified as "one of the children" whose troubles certainly cannot be serious aside from injuries and infections. A student in a school or college away from his home should investigate the health service of his institution and develop contacts with its physicians with the goal in mind of preventing ill health as well as having someone to consult if illness occurs.

Aside from questions of serious personal import for which one may want to consult a physician, there are a few easily recognizable danger signs or symptoms to which every person should respond. If the habit could be established early in life of seeking help when any of these symptoms appear, many lives would be saved or prolonged. The signals which should always prompt a person to secure competent advice include bleeding from an unusual source, a persistent lump or swelling, a lesion or sore which does not heal promptly, pain without obvious cause, unexplained weight loss or gain, and sudden loss of appetite. Indeed, any unusual development in body functioning should lead to appropriate investigation unless the reasons for it are obvious.

"I must be psychosomatic" is a common statement made by people who suffer from symptoms which come and go without much progression and usually without apparent cause. Such people are indeed psychosomatic, since mind and body function as a unit. It is only in discussions of the interaction between them that we sometimes discern each separately, and this is done only for purposes of clarity. Unfortunately, in seeking clear explanations as to how the body works, some people manage to convey the erroneous idea that mind and body are two separate entities co-operating with each other as best they can. For many people the term psychosomatic refers solely to disorders brought about by emotional stress. In fact, all diseases are psychosomatic. It is impossible to have a physical disorder without the emotions becoming involved, just as it is impossible to have emotional reactions without having some physiological reaction.

The body does have favorite ways of reminding its possessor that emotional strain is becoming burdensome. Sometimes the warning signal is headache or dizziness; at other times it may be nausea, vomiting, or diarrhea. Sleeplessness, fatigue, or apathy may indicate undue stress. Indeed, the variety of symptoms resulting from stress is almost endless.

Fear is an emotion which almost everyone understands out of

his own experience. Something threatens us, and we respond by trying to avoid the obvious danger. Our bodies undergo a series of changes causing alertness, thus enabling us to fight or run away, whichever seems appropriate. But often the source of uneasiness is not clear, and in such instances the unpleasant feelings of anticipation or dread are called anxiety. For most people, anxiety is harder to bear than fear, because they think little can be done about it. Those individuals who can keep busy suffer less from either fear or anxiety than those who must remain inactive.

Chronic anxiety may be influential in producing peptic ulcers, colitis, various allergic disorders, particularly asthma, high blood pressure, proneness to accidents and many other disorders. It is no disgrace to have these or any other symptoms resulting from emotional conflict, but it is sheer foolishness to avoid talking freely and frankly with one's physician as a means of getting rid of them.

If the desire for good health becomes so strong in an individual that he thinks of little else, he suffers from hypochondriasis. This in itself is as much of a disease as the conditions which such a person is trying to avoid. Dr. Edward Churchill, the surgical chief at the Massachusetts General Hospital, has said that "the quest for individual survival in this world is fully as intense as the older hope for personal immortality in the next." Somewhere between hypochondriasis and utter heedlessness lies the proper path to optimum health.

Motivation is one of the main factors on which good health depends, but proper motivation is largely dependent on how one thinks of his body. Many people are so accustomed to think in mechanical terms, accustomed as they are to automobiles and other products of our technological age, that they conceive of their bodies as machines with a certain expected life span and with individual parts which may be removed or replaced when they do not function properly. They assume that any abuses of the body can always be corrected. It is only a small step to the assumption that the usual laws of nature do not apply to them —the myth of invincibility.

Years ago Dr. Walter Cannon elaborated a theory of total integration of body functioning, the maintenance of internal balance, which he called homeostasis. Where the body is seriously threatened a huge variety of correcting devices come into play. For example, under ordinary circumstances blood clots in one to five minutes, but after the loss of several pints it will clot in a few seconds. The body can adapt itself to extremely dry climates, high altitudes and severe exercise. But pushing such changes too far and too fast may result in irreversible changes. In a sense, every intelligent person should be a student of his own capacities and limitations, even though an amateur, and try to live productively within them. In this way, he may learn to co-operate wisely with his own natural regulating processes, which are vital to the maintenance of good health.

Every person encounters numerous threats to health throughout life. We will now discuss some of those of most importance to young adults.

INFECTIONS

The Common Cold

The common cold continues to be a nuisance to people of all ages. In spite of numerous "cures" that have been reported over the last few decades, colds are still with us and probably will continue to be for a long time to come. Colds are caused by a filterable virus, perhaps a half-dozen or more varieties, but no dependable vaccine has yet been developed. When body resistance has been lowered by a cold, secondary invasion by bacteria is common, giving rise to sore throats, sinus and ear infections, and infections of the trachea, bronchi and smaller lung structures. No specific treatment for colds has yet been devised.

A few general principles concerning the management of colds have been established, however, which if practiced would result in considerably reduced suffering.

1. Go to bed as soon as a cold begins and stay there for one to three days. If this is impossible, stay in bed during all but the absolutely necessary working hours.
2. Drink as much water or fruit juices as you can imbibe comfortably.
3. Avoid chilling; hot baths are excellent to promote comfort if one does not get cold afterward.
4. Always use handkerchiefs or paper tissues to prevent spreading your infection to others. One unmuffled sneeze projects thousands of droplets into the air, each containing the infective virus, for others to breathe.
5. Keep the use of nose drops to a minimum. Using a very thick pillow with the obstructed nostril uppermost often relieves obstruction. Fortunately, colds usually have the habit of affecting one side of the nasal passages at a time, particularly in the early stages.

Some persons get relief from the use of pain-relieving compounds containing an antihistaminic drug. Used sparingly only when secretions are excessive, these may relieve symptoms and do no harm. They will not affect the length or severity of a cold. Antibiotics do a simple cold no good, and their uncritical use is to be condemned.

Many people demand that their physician give them penicillin when they have colds, and unfortunately some physicians do not resist such pressures. The old adage that he who treats himself has a fool for a doctor is quite applicable here.

A very compelling reason for treating all colds with respect is that many other infections may be indistinguishable from colds in their early stages. Measles, German measles, chicken-pox, whooping cough, influenza, cerebrospinal fever, and virus pneumonia are among the most common of these. If one manages himself intelligently, as suggested above, he may prevent these diseases from becoming as serious as might otherwise be the case. With good management, the patient will be under good treatment for a day or more before the characteristic symptoms appear and thus the worse effects of these illnesses may be avoided.

A few very serious diseases, acute nephritis and rheumatic fever being prime examples, often occur a few days or weeks after respiratory infections in which bacteria of the hemolytic streptococci type have been involved. Once these diseases have become established, through mechanisms not yet perfectly understood, elimination of the hemolytic streptococci, if still present, does no good. Prevention of the original infection is all that would have helped in a major way. This is all the greater reason why mild infections should receive prompt and appropriate treatment, particularly bed rest. As housing and sanitary standards improve and good health habits are acquired, such diseases become less common in the general population.

Fresh Air

One of the inheritances from the past that is open to grave question is the idea that one should sleep with windows open throughout the year, insuring plenty of fresh air. Obviously, everyone needs fresh air, awake or asleep, but the virtue of excessively cold air in the bedroom in promoting health is very limited. On the contrary, such cold air may cause chilling and irritation of the trachea and bronchi, and thus give rise to increased rather than decreased respiratory infections. Sleeping quarters should be well ventilated, but it is preferable for the contrast in temperature between day and night living conditions to be only a few degrees. The theory that the body is "hardened" by frequent exposure to violent extremes of weather has not been proven.

Infectious Mononucleosis

Wherever large groups of young people work together, there is always some concern and occasional discussion of a disease which usually afflicts a few of them each year. Though seldom a threat to life, it is troublesome because it slows its victims down, causing them to work inefficiently for several days or at times for a few weeks. This disease is infectious mononucleosis, usually known as "mono," or by some other short descriptive name.

The cause of this disorder is unknown. A filterable virus is probably responsible, but this has not been proved. Even the method of transmission is not certain, in spite of many theories developed on every college campus. It seems to be more common among interns, nurses, college students and others who are grouped in various institutions. This probably is due to the fact that, because these individuals are subject to better medical supervision than most people, the diagnosis is more readily made when they become ill. The average person who has a sore throat, a period of easy fatigability and a variety of none-too-serious symptoms will usually not have a blood count, whereas those persons who are near laboratories will do so. The usual symptoms of malaise, sore throat, fever, and slight enlargement of lymph nodes last from a few days to two or three weeks. Headache and lack of appetite are sometimes present. In addition to examining blood smears, a special "heterophile agglutination test" is helpful in making the diagnosis. Although mononucleosis can be accompanied by a number of complications, the great majority of cases recover without them. A person who has this disorder should rest when fatigued, follow his physician's instructions, and usually should not become involved in contact sports during his period of convalescence because of the danger of rupture of the spleen. Much has been said about the complications of infectious mononucleosis and as a result many people suffer more than is necessary simply because they fear that something may happen or because they have been told that they should be depressed or below par for several weeks or months. Although there is no specific treatment, close supervision by a skilled physician who treats the symptoms and complications by non-specific measures practically always leads to complete recovery. Dropping out of school or college is usually not necessary or desirable. (A "specific" treatment refers to a drug or other agent uniquely effective against the organism which causes the illness, for example, penicillin for pneumonia caused by pneumococcus bacteria.)

German Measles

Most of the ordinary communicable diseases of childhood have a high nuisance value and some, notably whooping cough, may be fatal. One of them, German measles, has a particular and unique hazard. If this occurs in a woman in the first third of her pregnancy, the possibilities of fetal abnormalities are somewhat increased. These may be of almost any nature, ranging all the way from stillbirth to defects of the eyes, ears, heart, and blood vessels or mental retardation. Since the disease itself is very mild and its serious complications are very rare, it is desirable that all girls have the disease before marriage. However, medical and college authorities are reticent about urging that female students deliberately expose themselves to the disease. When German measles does occur in early pregnancy, an experienced specialist should be consulted. Women who are members of religious bodies that do not condone termination of pregnancy should be consoled by remembering that if they contract German measles they have about nine chances out of ten of having a normal baby, according to recent studies.

Boils and Carbuncles

A boil is an infection of the skin, usually occurring on the face, neck, forearms, underarms, and the upper part of the back. Carbuncles are essentially boils with multiple foci and are usually present on the back of the neck or back. Most infections begin with a small pustule at the base of a hair follicle. They are usually due to staphylococci. One should be particularly careful not to squeeze boils either in their early or late stages. Sometimes a single boil is followed by several others in the surrounding skin due to direct spread of the infective agent. Treatment is then a matter for a physician to suggest, and one should always seek help if it is at all possible. Antibiotics may be used, but only under a physician's direction. Ointments containing antibiotics may be put on the skin around the boils to prevent spread. Prevention is a difficult problem. A person with boils should handle himself with great care to prevent giving them to other persons. This care should extend to bed clothing, underwear, handkerchiefs, shirts, and any material which may be exposed to the lesion. Frequent hand washing is particularly desirable during this period. Boils around the nose and lips are especially dangerous and should be treated with great care since squeezing or any trauma may cause infection to spread inside the cranial cavity. Hot compresses are useful in hastening the localization of boils.

Venereal Diseases

The venereal diseases, of which syphilis and gonorrhea are by far the most important, were formerly looked upon as so disgraceful that their names could not even be mentioned publicly, nor could informative articles about them be published in newspapers and magazines. During the last three decades all this has changed, and they can be discussed freely. In the meantime, the development of an effective antibiotic (penicillin) against them has helped to reduce the incidence of both diseases to a marked degree. However, this has resulted in a false sense of security on the part of many persons, and as a result, in many sections of the country, venereal diseases are again increasing in frequency. Although public reticence about syphilis and gonorrhea has in part disappeared, private sensitivity concerning their presence persists relatively unchanged. The result is that many persons who contract these diseases avoid going to a competent physician, fearing disclosure. Instead they accept advice from persons who have no accurate knowledge of the treatment or complications of these conditions. This is truly a tragic situation, since both gonorrhea and syphilis are easily and effectively stopped by proper dosages of penicillin, but if untreated or improperly treated their aftereffects and complications may be very distressing indeed. In these disorders perhaps more than in any others, the advice to consult your physician early should always be followed.

Athlete's Foot

The fungus infection known as epidermophytosis, or more commonly as "athlete's foot," is so prevalent as to be well-nigh universal. Treatment of the acute manifestations should be prescribed by a physician according to the nature, site, degree and complications of the lesions. Prevention is largely up to the individual, guided by suggestions from professional sources.

The favored sites for the organism to flourish are those which are moist, such as between the toes. A cardinal point in discouragement of fungus is dryness. Therefore, any procedures which encourage dryness and cleanliness are effective in prevention of infection. Shoes should be allowed to dry out thoroughly between wearings, socks should be washed daily, and powder should be dusted between the toes frequently, preferably after bathing. Ordinary talcum powder is helpful, but a special preparation containing undecylenic acid and zinc undecylenate (Desenex) is even more effective, since it contains an active fungicidal agent. For many people who have had the infection there is no such a thing as a cure. Instead there is only a kind of symbiotic relationship in which the organism is apparently kept in a subdued and quiescent state, only to increase to the symptom forming stage when preventive procedures are relaxed or omitted.

Many people are lulled into a false sense of security when they see foot baths in the shower rooms which they use. These may have some effectiveness, but only when the fungicidal agent is present in sufficient concentration and if it is changed two or three times a week, or even oftener if use is excessive. In the Harvard University Field House a one per cent solution of sodium hypochloride is the fungicidal agent in use.

SPECIAL HEALTH TOPICS

Epilepsy

There is no problem in the health field that is apt to cause so much anxiety and lead to so many unnecessary fears as epilepsy.

There are two main kinds: the so-called "grand mal" (in which classification 60 per cent of all cases fall), and "petit mal," which accounts for the rest. The former is easy to identify, because its characteristic symptom is a generalized convulsive seizure. The latter may be very mild, with inconspicuous signs or symptoms such as the omission of a word in conversation, dropping an object from the hand, or a tiny flicker of the eyes or eyelids.

There is another variety called *psychomotor epilepsy*. This may take the form of some kind of socially unacceptable behavior, outbursts of anger or episodes of rage which do not seem to have appropriate provocation.

Epilepsy may be caused by some unusual structure, such as a vascular anomaly, a tumor, or atrophy of brain cells, or it may be caused by a chemical change such as too much calcium or too little sugar in the blood. Brain damage in early life may also produce epilepsy. In any case, disturbances of consciousness should always be investigated to find the cause. In those instances in which no apparent cause can be found, the individual is said to have "idiopathic" epilepsy, a scientific way of saying the cause is hidden or unknown.

In recent years a variety of medications have been developed which will control the seizures in whole or in part without seriously affecting cerebral functioning. Phenobarbital is one of the oldest and most economical of these. Others are dilantin, mysoline, tridione, milontin, and a multiplicity of newer drugs.

Numerous questions arise with a person who has epilepsy. Should he be allowed to drive a car? Should he take part in athletics? What kinds of jobs may he hold? How about military service? Should a person with epilepsy marry? The laws of some states are very unrealistic in these respects. A few forbid marriage of any persons with epilepsy, with no clear definition of what is meant by the term and no distinction between the various types and grades of severity. Such laws are, of course, evaded and become only a source of disrespect for law generally.

In Massachusetts a person with epilepsy may be permitted to drive provided he remains under treatment and has been seizure-free for eighteen consecutive months. Persons with epilepsy under control should go to school and hold jobs just like everyone else, with sensible precautions about working in high places or under circumstances of potentially extreme hazard to others.

Epilepsy should not be a bar to marriage. The chance of a person's passing epilepsy on to his children is relatively slight, possibly 1 in 40, but the possibility is much increased if both partners have the disorder.

Abstention from alcohol is desirable. When a person with epilepsy obtains a job, he should remain under medical supervision, tell his employer or prospective employer the truth about himself and at the same time be prepared occasionally to encounter prejudiced attitudes on the part of some of them.

About 800,000 people in the United States have such disturbances of consciousness. Serious mental deterioration is unusual in epilepsy. Intelligence of epileptics ranges from defective to very superior, just as in the rest of the population. Fear of seizures may cause more suffering than the seizures themselves. Most people need help for the emotional problems that are so prevalent among those who have the disease.

The Thyroid

The thyroid gland is frequently a source of much interest to those who have symptoms that are vague and ill defined, and as a consequence many persons are told that the source of their difficulties is in thyroid dysfunction, whereas in fact it is functioning quite normally. Diseases of the thyroid are relatively common, and for most of them treatment is effective. The thyroid may be overactive (hyperthyroidism), underactive (hypothyroidism, myxedema), inflamed (thyroiditis), or enlarged due to lack of iodine (goiter); or it may develop nodules, some of which may be malignant. All these conditions and their various modifications require accurate, specific treatment, and competent physicians can make the proper diagnosis. A most troublesome situation arises when a student who is not doing well in school is told that his thyroid is at fault because the basal metabolic rate is "a little high" or "lower than average." Determining the rate of metabolism is just one, and not the most important, of a variety of procedures designed to diagnose disorders of the thyroid. It suffers the disadvantage that there is a wide normal range and that subjective factors such as emotional tension may make significant alterations in the reading. Under some circumstances it may be useful or even essential in a series of diagnostic procedures, but when a moderate variation in the basal metabolic rate is the only sign of consequence, factors other than disordered thyroid function should be considered. Many a student with an emotional problem has been treated for months for a slightly abnormal "BMR" when it was totally unnecessary and even harmful, since it prevented appropriate investigation of the true handicap.

Radiation

As a result of controversies over nuclear weapon testing and the resulting fall-out of radioactive material, many people are intensely concerned about the total amount of radiation to which they are exposed. This is a proper attitude, provided that one does not let the fear of radioactive energy prevent the proper use of it when it may prolong life. Radiation reaches us from a variety of "natural" substances and from cosmic rays, through the machines used in medical and dental diagnosis, radioisotopes used in medical treatment, laboratory experiments and some industrial processes, and from the fall-out resulting from testing atomic and thermonuclear weapons. Radioactive wastes from atomic power plants are an additional potential hazard.

A good principle to keep in mind is that any unnecessary exposure to sources of radioactivity is undesirable, particularly in young people. Excessive radiation may be of importance in the production of leukemia and cancer, but for the young person the possible effect on reproductive cells is of greatest importance. Mutations in germ cells, with resultant defects in children, are possibilities which we most wish to avoid.

The body is readily capable of tolerating a considerable amount of radiation. If this were not true we should all perish. Many threats to health, namely tuberculosis, dental abscesses, new growths in all parts of the body, ulcers and other lesions of the intestinal tract, and many other conditions can be recognized only by the use of still more radiation in the form of medical X-rays. For the person with a medical problem, the question that should be considered is: Which is likely to be most harmful, the possible disease which may be diagnosed by means of X-rays, or the radiation used in the process? In almost all instances, the answer will be that the risk from the potential disease to be diagnosed is far greater than that from the radiation. A proper course of action for an individual interested in maintaining his own health is to ask questions about shielding of X-ray equipment and to seek enough additional information to confirm his confidence in his physician, after which he should undertake the tests which have been recommended for him. Any physician worth consulting will be very well aware of these considerations, and he will expect you to be concerned about them too. There is no point, however, in consulting a physician and then refusing to have the tests necessary for proper diagnosis. One should be sure his physician knows what he is doing and then do what he suggests.

Smoking

Discussion of this topic has become so controversial and so widespread that it seems to be an additional advertisement for the tobacco industry. At any rate, the consumption of tobacco increases year by year. For many young people smoking is not only a status symbol, signifying that one has grown up, but also a means of irritating or embarrassing one's parents. Unfortunately, once one has become addicted to tobacco (acquired the habit), it is very difficult to stop using it. From a practical standpoint, the only time one really has a free choice is before one starts using it.

Coincident with the increasingy frequent use of tobacco, cancer of the lung has become more common until it is now the most frequent cause of death from cancer among men in many regions. It is about six times more prevalent in men than in women. Many theories have been advanced as to the reason, but the most convincing ones center around the large amounts of irritating (perhaps cancerogenic) substances introduced into the lungs under conditions of modern life. Before the discovery of bacteria, the gastrointestinal tract was thought to be the chief sufferer from the introduction of harmful substances into the body. We now understand the harmful effects of spoiled foods and contamination from carriers of gastrointestinal diseases and can largely avoid them, but we have a new hazard. As urban centers become larger and industrialized, the air is polluted by smoke, dust, engine gases, and other materials, sometimes to such a degree that comfortable breathing becomes impossible. The term smog has been applied to such a polluted atmosphere, and for some cities the smog problem is their greatest health hazard. If the inhalation of tobacco smoke is now added to all the other substances inhaled involuntarily, the capacity of lung tissue to protect itself from cancerous growths may be impaired. Absolute proof that smoking causes lung cancer, which will convince those who have vested interests to protect, is still lacking. The stubborn coincidence that heavy smokers are about twenty times more likely to develop lung cancer than non-smokers is a very impressive one. For the present, the burden of proof lies with those who claim that heavy smoking and lung cancer have nothing to do with one another.

Equally disturbing to those who aspire to live as long as possible are the epidemiological studies suggesting that the longevity of heavy smokers is less by several years than that of abstainers.

Each young person should weigh these considerations carefully while he has the freedom of judgment to determine for himself whether smoking is worth the possible consequences about which health officials are so much concerned.

Alcohol

Almost anything that one can say about alcohol as a health hazard is likely to provoke heated criticism from someone. Anyone with a highly developed capacity for indignation can become very agitated over the evils of alcohol. If his sense of realism is not particularly acute, he may come to the conclusion that the problem can be solved only by eliminating alcohol or forbidding its use. This "noble experiment" has been tried, and it seems unlikely that this nation will try it again. Yet alcoholism, one of our greatest social problems, as it is in various other countries, is probably on the increase. Occasional groups in our country, motivated by the highest sentiments, have from time to time, forbidden the use of alcohol by their members, only to find that those who break over in moments of desperation use far more than they would have consumed had the negative pressures not been so strong originally. It is a moot question at times as to whether alcohol or a rigidly intolerant attitude about it does the most harm to the individual.

Chronic alcoholism is that condition in which a person can consume no alcohol without undergoing marked changes in his behavior. The chronic alcoholic relies on alcohol, is unable to stop using it, uses it to an extent which interferes with his own life and the comfort of those around him, and is unable or unwilling to recognize these facts about himself. In short, he is an ill person, usually with deep-seated psychological problems for which the drinking is an inappropriate and ineffective solution. It takes more than alcohol to produce a chronic alcoholic.

Some institutions attempt to solve the problems created by alcohol by passing rules forbidding its use. Since these rules frequently cannot be enforced, elaborate methods of circumventing them may be developed, some of which actually bring prestige to the rule-breakers. Those who made the rules feel virtuous; those who break them with impunity are satisfied, and only those whose duty it is to enforce the rules see that the institution has, with the best of intent, developed a way of creating hypocrisy and disrespect for law.

So far as is known, no school, college or other institution has ever evolved an entirely satisfactory solution to the alcohol problem. A preferable approach is one in which drinking is not separated out as a special problem, but is considered in the total context of individual behavior. Improper behavior when an individual is drinking is not excused. No exception is made for the offending person who operates a motor car improperly or who does not live up to the standards expected of him in college or industry. Most physicians consider that alcohol is not harmful to those who can use it in moderation, who know when it must not be used, and who are not dependent on it. He who needs it should not use it.

Cerebral Stimulants

Young people are prone to use cerebral stimulants of various kinds when they are under stress, or anticipate that they will be. Among the most common of these are benzedrine and caffeine, the latter frequently in the form of pills sold in drug stores and sometimes by unscrupulous vendors under a variety of trade names. Benzedrine and its derivatives often constitute the active ingredient in "pep pills" used by unethical athletes.

The use of these substances before periods of intense study, examinations or strenuous athletic performances should be condemned without reservation. They may improve performance temporarily, but the after-effects are frequently quite deplorable. Students often require hospitalization to recover from the over-stimulating qualities of these drugs, and athletes have been known to lose their lives from the improper use of such stimulants. Their use is a mark of bad judgment and desperation at best, and at worst they serve as vehicles of exploitation of some human beings by others who are completely unscrupulous. Many young men and women who are struggling with the common emotional conflicts involved in emancipating themselves from home and establishing themselves as individuals with a separate identity think it sophisticated to explore the effects of such drugs as peyote (mescaline), marihuana, or opium and its derivatives. Such experimentation is very dangerous, and those who use their intelligence will not indulge in it.

The Skin

The skin is one of the most versatile organs of the body, though not so complicated as the liver or the bone marrow. It acts as a thermostat to keep the body at an agreeable temperature, secretes and excretes water, oils, and various solids, protects all the more sensitive body structures, and renews itself constantly and automatically. Many people believe that a well-tanned skin is an indicator of good health, whereas it only protects one from more than the usual exposure to sunlight. Excessive exposure to sunlight with periodic sunburn may lead to skin cancer. Since the skin contains oil glands, and these often become temporarily overactive during puberty, obstruction and infection occur frequently, causing acne, the most common of all skin disorders. When an oil gland becomes clogged with dead skin cells, hardened oil, dirt and bacteria, a blackhead or a pimple is the result. These should never be squeezed. Frequent washing with plenty of soap is usually helpful, and physicians may suggest combinations of chemicals which will aid in keeping the oil glands open. A temporary imbalance of hormone production usually underlies severe acne, but the exact nature of the disorder is not understood clearly enough as yet to warrant hormone treatment.

In early life the skin is soft and flexible. In middle and old age it becomes less elastic and drier, and develops wrinkles. No procedures or substances will keep the skin youthful, though many women spend millions of dollars for them, thinking they are doing so. Moles on the skin are usually harmless, but if they become irritated, are situated at points of continual friction, or grow darker and bleed occasionally they should be removed at once by surgical excision. Warts are caused by a virus and usually disappear spontaneously. The skin is very sensitive to a variety of body conditions, and hence its color or appearance may tell an experienced observer much about the body's general condition.

The Teeth

About 95 per cent of all people suffer at some time in their lives from decayed teeth. It is estimated that at any given time among the people in the United States there are about a billion cavities which should be filled. Yet there is no physiological reason why any person should not keep his teeth throughout his lifetime. The teeth are living structures, constantly exchanging minerals with the rest of the body. Unlike other body structures, however, once decay starts the process never becomes arrested. Only the removal of the affected portion and substitution of an artificial substance stops decay. There are simply not enough dentists to treat all the teeth that are diseased, even if their owners could afford it. Prevention of tooth decay is, therefore, the only present hope of saving teeth for the majority of our people. Diet is of great importance in preventing tooth decay. Cleaning the teeth immediately after eating is also of great importance. Research with "trace" elements in the body has revealed that one of them, fluoride, is necessary for sound teeth. Fluoride enters into a chemical reaction at the surfaces of the enamel, forming a relatively insoluble compound which enables the teeth to resist decay. If there is too little fluoride, the teeth decay readily. If there is too much, the enamel becomes very hard and undergoes a brownish mottled discoloration, but does not decay. About one part of fluoride to a million parts of water is the most desirable concentration. At this level no harm results to the body, and tooth decay is reduced about 65 per cent. The cost is about 10 cents per person per year.

For a variety of reasons, this method of reducing dental cares has been the subject of all sorts of emotional reactions, causing much controversy in nearly every city or town in which fluoridation of water has been proposed. It does not seem likely, however, that the forces which oppose furnishing our children with appropriate minerals for developing strong and healthy bodies will prevail in the long run, particularly in view of the lack of evidence that fluoride in appropriate amounts is harmful.

The person who refuses dental X-rays because of fear of excess radiation, when they are clearly indicated for purposes of diagnosis, is using short-sighted judgment. The harm to the body from an abscessed tooth or the possible loss of a tooth from a process not visible to oral examination is far greater than the potential harm from radiation.

Tooth health and comfort are likely to be at their best when the individual respects his teeth as he should respect his heart, cleans them regularly and properly, pays attention to his diet, supports public health measures designed to reduce tooth decay, visits his dentist regularly, and follows his instructions.

Conserving Vision and Hearing

The average young person usually sees little connection between his own health habits and the instances of visual and auditory difficulties he sees every day in older people. Most cases of partial or complete blindness or of hearing loss were not inevitable—they have resulted from accidents and illnesses that were theoretically preventable. Obviously, accidents and illnesses cannot be entirely avoided. If individual episodes causing permanent harm to someone can be prevented, surely the total number of such unfortunate occurrences could be reduced if everyone were careful. Conservation of sight and hearing is peculiarly dependent upon good health habits when one is young.

Vision is most apt to be preserved if one gets adequate sleep, avoids using the eyes for close work under conditions that bring discomfort, wears goggles when working with machinery that may throw foreign bodies into the eyes, and gets adequate treatment early for any infection or other disorder. Routine use of eye drops or washes is undesirable. Those who are nearsighted or farsighted, or who have astigmatism or other visual problems, should select a good ophthalmologist and follow his instructions. An ophthalmologist is a physician who specializes in disorders of the eyes.

Since deafness so often results from a long series of infections of the nose, throat, sinuses, and ear, special precaution to minimize the severity of such infections is of the utmost importance. Working near sources of loud noise with ear plugs is another source of hearing loss. Occasionally a person invests in a hearing device without having had a thorough examination by a competent physician only to find later that his disability was not one that could be helped by a hearing aid. Occasionally accumulation of wax interferes with hearing, and its removal restores normal function.

Diet and Exercise

These subjects are the excuse for dissemination of enormous amounts of misinformation, whether in schools and colleges or in the sports page of newspapers. All too many persons proceed on the theory that if some of these commodities are good, even more must be better.

The average healthy young man or woman should have a balanced diet, one that contains enough calories, minerals, and vitamins to enable his body to function properly. Fortunately, these requirements are automatically met if the individual eats some meat, green vegetables, and citrus fruits or tomatoes and drinks a pint or more of milk each day. The total amount can be gauged by appetite and weight level. For such an individual the addition of vitamins, gelatin, or products recommended by the food faddists, are of primary benefit to those who produce and sell these substances. They usually do no harm, but neither are they necessary.

In colleges, the supposed benefits of training tables for athletes are the subject of much discussion. As devices for boosting the morale of athletes and for maintaining discipline, they are undoubtedly effective. They also constitute a reward for services rendered. There is no scientific justification, from the standpoint of nutrition, for expensive steaks in contrast to more plebeian forms of protein. Therefore, arguments for training tables should be based on other grounds than that athletes need food of a different quality from that of other people. The mere physical task of imbibing enough calories for optimum performance in strenuous sports like football may call for added concentration—for example, it may be necessary for such an athlete to get up for breakfast if he is to eat all he may need during the day. The added costs of training tables has to be weighed against the psychological value of the ritual to athletes and to those who think well enough of the practice to bear the cost.

Exercise may be helpful or harmful to a person, depending upon how it is carried out. In general it is desirable for both physical and social reasons. Those forms which can be pursued consistently all one's life are to be preferred. Those sports which have a special value as exhibitions of skill are also highly desirable, so long as the participants are able to transfer to other types of activity when they can no longer play the organized forms. To be avoided is the practice of exercising exceedingly vigorously in youth only to become indolent in early middle life, allowing one's self to become obese and a vulnerable subject for diseases of the heart and blood vessels. Like many other things, exercise should be consistent throughout life if it is to be of maximum benefit. Two eminent physicians are known to the writer who have been arguing all their lives as to whether strenuous exercise or just the minimum exertion necessary to work effectively is the more conducive to long life. Both are 76 and in good health, and the argument is proceeding enthusiastically.

Obesity

For all practical purposes, the only way to get fat is to eat more food than one needs. Whereas many people in the world suffer grievously from malnutrition, the chief nutritional problem in the United States is obesity. This is essentially a matter of emotions. Simple enjoyment of foods high in caloric content is the forerunner of much overweight. Compensation for failure to obtain satisfaction in other ways is in back of many other persons' habit of overeating. It is readily understandable how much easier it is to tolerate anxiety and frustration when one's stomach feels tight and full. Hearing the fearful statistics about obesity seldom does the hearer any good. Developing more appropriate personal satisfactions to replace those gained from overeating is frequently constructive. This process usually involves psychiatric treatment and is neither simple nor easy. Psychotherapy is practically never so.

Mortality rates for obese persons are about 50 per cent higher than for those of average weight or below. The greater the percentage of overweight the greater the mortality. Heart disease, cirrhosis of the liver, gallstones, high blood pressure, and especially diabetes are among the diseases which occur with more than average frequency in obese persons. The risk of surgical procedures is much greater when one is overweight.

It is easier to develop food habits in early life to avoid gaining undersirable weight than to reduce after one has become obese. Those advertisements which claim that if one uses a certain product it is possible to eat all one wants of any food and still lose weight either are falsehoods or they are pushing a product that is harmful to health. Older persons need fewer calories than young people and should eat less. Fortunately, most people are properly guided by their appetites as they grow older, but some are not.

Some people can reduce if they have to pay for the privilege, but cannot bring themselves to eat less butter, cream, rich gravies, fried foods, and rich desserts without such a stimulus.

Constipation

Constipation is the cause of much anxiety on the part of many people, and most of it is unnecessary. In the great majority of healthy persons, the bowels will take care of themselves providing the individuals will give them a chance. This means going to the toilet regularly and without undue hurry (after breakfast is one of the best times), eating a balanced diet, drinking considerable water daily, and avoiding preoccupation with the size or consistency of fecal material. Some people have bowel movements several times daily, others once or twice a week. There is no evidence that normal material has any toxins which are absorbed into other parts of the body if the bowels are not emptied promptly.

Laxatives should be avoided unless suggested or prescribed by a competent physician. Constipation, diarrhea, and abdominal pain are delicate indicators of disease, and when any sudden change or new development occurs a medical consultation is desirable. One should never take a laxative because of abdominal pain unless the source of the pain is known and the laxative is prescribed. An appendix which has become infected may easily be ruptured by such a dangerous procedure.

Obviously, a complete treatise on human physiology and how to avoid making the most common mistakes in health maintenance is not possible within the confines of a single chapter. The issues which have been discussed are those which have arisen most commonly in the writer's experience of nearly three decades of caring for young men and women in camps, colleges, and the armed services.

If you have learned that prevention is less expensive than disease or injury, that early consultation with your favorite physician may save much pain or disability, and that each person should be a student of his own body and how to protect it, reading this chapter will have been worthwhile and, for many of you, will result in the prolongation of your own life.

Becoming the Complete Adult
Emotionally

YOUR
BASIC
PSYCHOLOGY

by O. Spurgeon English, M.D., Professor and
Head of the Department of Psychiatry and Director of the Institute for the Study of Psychotherapy, Temple University Medical Center

and

Francis H. Hoffman, M.D., Clinical Professor
of Psychiatry, Director of Residency Training,
Co-Director of the Comprehensive Medicine
Clinic, Temple University Medical Center

2

You are unique; there is no one exactly like you anywhere in the world. You might well ask then, "How can anything written by someone who doesn't actually know me help me to know my self?" The answer is that what is written in this chapter and those that follow is about the things we share in common. Knowing more about these things that are shared helps us to identify our uniqueness. This gives us a better chance to strengthen the characteristics that we find to be good in ourselves.

THREE KINDS OF BASIC FEELINGS

What are these common experiences of life that we share with each other? Let us begin by noting that there are three things that are true about everybody: first, we all have dependency feelings—that is, we were born with and for the rest of our lives will have a need to be able to turn trustingly to others and rely upon them. Second, we all have feelings of aggression or ambition. Each of us is driven not only to protect himself from danger but also to strive to achieve. Third, we all have sexual feelings. These feelings are the motive force behind our wish for tenderness, closeness, affection, and love.

Our failure to straightforwardly face these facts may cause a great deal of conflict. In each of these areas there is much good, but too often we focus on the negative aspects of these feelings and feel shamefaced, anxious, or guilty about them. We very often try to repress—that is, push out of our awareness—the fact of these feelings, and when we do, we create a jack-in-the-box. Anyone can trigger the catch and make these feelings spring up before us without a moment's warning. We ourselves, by relaxing the constant vigilance which repression requires, may trigger the catch.

Our Feelings of Dependency

Let us look at our dependency feelings on a simple biological level. Each night we must return to a dependent, supine position, in which we try to lay aside the care and conflict of the day and restore our strength. We need to sleep, and during sleep we rely heavily upon others to take care of us. In less complicated times, for example, a watchman would call out the hours regularly to let people know that all was well. Now, we rely upon others to heat our homes and to provide us with water, electricity, and many other things. The range of our dependent needs increases with increasing specialization. This is a fact that makes many of us uncomfortable. Many people bemoan the fact that we are no longer a nation of rugged individualists, each dependent mostly upon himself. We could, of course, become so by retiring to a wood as Thoreau briefly did. We would thus limit our expectations and limit the richness that life can provide us through the social system of interpersonal dependency.

To depend upon others willingly and wisely is not a burden, but a source of strength. It enables each of us to attack our daily tasks with more freedom and imagination than we would otherwise be capable of, if we attempted the near-impossibility of extreme self-sufficiency.

Our Feelings of Aggression

We know that life itself depends upon a willingness to face difficulties and strife, and overcome them. Life is composed of organisms ranging from the very nearly inanimate submicroscopic viral organisms to ourselves, and from there perhaps to the macroscopic life of the universe. In this scheme, each organism lives on the basis of controlling and feeding upon other organisms which provide it with the energy of life. Species survival depends upon the efficiency of this primitive aggressive control. This is not something that we ordinarily like to think about. Indeed, there are the vegetarians who try to abandon this feeding aggression entirely.

The drive to achieve, succeed, and move ahead in life is as essential to life as nourishment itself. Even acquiring control over our own acquisitive desires requires a self-directed aggression, which we call self-discipline. To give an example from Dr. Paul Wilcox, we can equate our elemental aggressiveness with an explosion of gasoline. If gasoline explodes on the sidewalk where there are people, it may well kill or maim, and we rightly say that this is destructive. However, when we put the same explosion in the cylinder of an automobile engine and explode it synchronously with other explosions in other cylinders, what results is not something destructive, but a force which can move us from place to place. The essential factor is not the aggressive explosive force itself, but what use is made of it.

Our Feelings of Sexuality

Without the biologically based feelings of sexuality which we share in common with all other human beings, our species would shortly be extinct. Occasionally we hear of groups of people whose cultural customs and taboos have precluded their continuance as a member of the species. Ringed with fear and superstition, yet apparently unknowingly, they are proceeding to extinction.

The obvious biological utility of sexual feelings has not prevented human beings from trying to rid themselves of the awareness of these feelings. This attempt has unfortunately resulted in a complicated problem. Attempts to deny the reality of these feelings make control more difficult. Dr. Herman Bundesen, the public health officer of Chicago who did yeoman work with the venereal diseases, did so by getting their existence publicly recognized so that effective preventive and control measures could be instituted. On a very basic level, all our responses to the world around us and our feelings about it can be called sexual, since everyone is a sexually defined human being, that is, male or female.

It is important, then, that we recognize that we do have dependent, aggressive, and sexual feelings. Of course, how we respond to and handle these feelings will depend a good deal upon our environment and the people around us from whom we learned to control them. Failure to recognize that these feelings are a part of life puts us in the position of a family at dinner when a burglar comes in through the dining room window. If they try to repress, to hide from themselves, to deny the fact of the existence of the burglar, he can go around the table picking up the silverware and leave them without the tools with which to eat. They can, of course, resort to fingers and pull the roast apart instead of carving it, but how much simpler it would be if they had not pretended the burglar was invisible or not there. When they saw him coming through the window, they could have called the police, asked him what he was doing there, and actually stopped him from taking the things that they needed. They might even have converted him to some beneficial use to society, and thereby to themselves.

If we were born as other animals and insects, with an innate patterning that our future lives would follow, our biology itself would direct how these feelings would be utilized. Everyone can agree that there is a tremendous efficiency in the biological structuring of the instincts of bees and ants. In a colony of bees, only one of the many potential queen bees is allowed to survive. The ruthlessness of unalterable instinct is a fearsome thing. The concept that men by social institutions might try the same thing is a present-day nightmare. Aldous Huxley's *Brave New World* and George Orwell's *1984* are chronicles of fear of the potential development of our society in this direction. Perhaps there is some unformed remembrance of our evolutionary past which gives added meaning and fearfulness to such a possibility. In our lives we have many times had the feeling that we would rather have instinct control some of these feelings than have to deal with them with our minds. Certainly in spring, when the young man's and the young lady's fancies "lightly turn to thoughts of love" (although you know they do this all year), if they have to study for final examinations, they may wish that the intrusive romantic thoughts would disappear. So, too, at the time of examinations, they may wish that instead of having to compete and prove themselves they could go back to the good old days when the blacksmith's son became a blacksmith and the farmer's son became a farmer. But of course the peddler's son became a peddler and the beggar's son became a beggar.

As we gain an awareness that these feelings are universal, we are less likely to be disturbed by them. The fact that such opposing feelings as love and anger can coexist and be directed at the same person or event at the same time often confuses us.

One feeling can be so dominant that we may be unaware of the existence of the opposite. Sometimes they merge, as when love becomes bittersweet or a victory becomes Pyrrhic, gained at too great a cost to our other needs and feelings. We work to obtain a balance, and usually do. We learn ways to divert our aggression into creative channels and focus our love and dependency in areas and with people where it can be safely expressed. We retain, however, the awareness that these opposing needs and feelings still exist within us.

THE FORMATIVE YEARS—BIRTH TO AGE SEVEN

The Period of Natural Appetites

With only very basic biologic instincts to rely upon at birth, we all need a long period of experience and instruction. The human infant is carried inside its mother until the time for being born. Then a new world of experience bursts upon him. Immediate readjustments are made in his breathing and in his circulatory system.

Now he has to signal those around him with the only methods available to him: crying and threshing his arms and legs. He is unable to find a breast and nurse as do other animals. It must be given to him. Thus begins the period of natural appetites, as the infant uses his mouth as a means of investigation because of his primary need of being fed. If his wants were complex, they might be difficult to figure out, but a new baby's needs are relatively simple. He needs to be fed, kept warm, and caressed. But the satisfaction of these needs, if only done mechanically, would begin immediately to condition a zestless response to the world around him.

If our parents were cold, either because of their own natures or because they were following the dictates of some current theory of baby care, we may have acquired in us the seeds of desperation against which we have continually to fight in our later lives. It is surprising how many parents feel that they ought to permit frustration to continue, even at this early age. They sometimes begin worrying right away that their child will become spoiled unless they let him "cry it out" alone. There is so much in life that is really beyond our control that we ought to consider it essential to relieve any frustration that we can.

Children who are left to cry it out alone often grow up mistrustful of the people around them, and can never really believe that anyone will come to help them when they need it. Children who are left to be hungry until feeding time, or who differ from their parents' expectations of how much or how little food they should take, can develop into adults who can never be sure of getting enough food, or into adults who do not want to take food from anyone.

Certainly to every child, mother is the most important person in the first few years of life. But father ought not miss the opportunity of watching and feeling with this newly developing human being that is his. Doing things for the child gives him a chance to "lock in" and enjoy a very real relationship. If he does not, he may find later on that he may not have developed in his child the awareness of his love that makes all direction and discipline more easily understood and abided by.

The Period of Controlling

During this part of a child's development there is a major emphasis upon toilet training. The child is learning to do something, not because he wants to, but because someone else asks it of him. Any attempts at self-control are difficult for two reasons: One, this growing organism, changing each day, has only poor control over his basic body mechanisms. Two, the child has a low tolerance for frustration. If he fails after first attempts, he is likely to want to return to the earlier adjustment where less is required of him. Toilet success is not important to him. The amount of love and affection given him during the oral stage of development will determine how much frustration he can tolerate.

The ability to successfully meet the demands of toilet training gives a sense of independence and strength which is self-sustaining. This is, of course, not a development in a straight line, but one of alternating successes and failures. So long as the general direction is toward success, feelings of achievement and self-reliance are incorporated into the child's view of himself.

Many parents, oppressed by the conviction that their child must be toilet trained, begin early the gentle art of stool-catching. They watch closely, and when they see the strained look that signifies a bowel movement, they immediately snatch him and put him on the pot. Unfortunately the snatching experience is not very conducive to a relaxation of the rectal sphincter, so that an added complication of constipation may result. If, however, the parents are not too anxious about toilet training, or too harsh and strict in its enforcement, the child will usually co-operate willingly.

The two areas of taking in food and of complying with toilet training are ones where the child can easily defeat his parents. If they are strict in their demands to conform, the child can refuse food or, if it is forced down him, vomit it. Or he can hold in his bowel movements, suffering the pain of constipation but gaining a sense of independence and of successful rebellion. In school he may refuse to conform, and later in his job he may feel that to give anything to someone in authority, even so little a thing as a smile, might threaten him with a loss of his sense of independence. As an adult, he may have the fixed pattern of hurting himself in order to establish his sense of independence.

The child may give in to the demands of his parents and become exceptionally clean and neat. He takes in his parents' values and goes "whole hog." He cannot stand to be dirty in any way. He has a feeling of revulsion at the idea of any messiness. The middle ground of flexibility is always difficult, since it implies some need to shift our position as the situation requires. The unstably developing child often cannot tolerate even the small amount of anxiety this creates, so he seeks stability in a fixed position: either one thing or the other with no in-between.

A little compulsive neatness becomes a part of everyone's life pattern unless we have given up entirely the possibility of ever meeting those early standards which were so difficult to attain.

The successful resolution of the problems of control of bowel and bladder is the basis for a reasonable orderliness and a wish to meet our own standards as well as those of others. A warm relationship with our parents helps us incorporate their standards into ourselves and make them our own.

The feelings of inferiority which we all feel from time to time often have their basis in perceiving the control of our bodies to be almost insuperable. Comparison, with either older children or adults, makes our fumbling attempts at control seem ridiculous. We can always find someone better equipped to do things than we are ourselves. If the focus in our early toilet training is one of comparison with others, you can be sure that we will continue to find fault with ourselves even when it is totally unnecessary.

Even if comparisons are inescapable, we can learn to be accepting of our deficiencies. We can use them to measure ourselves by, in order to evaluate where we can make reasonable efforts to improve. If, every time you attempt this, you slide right into self-disparagement, your early efforts at self-control were not warmly enough encouraged. As we grow, we learn that unless our parents absolutely hated us they also had a stake in our success. Therefore we may use the mechanisms of failure and self-disparagement to get back at them for ways in which we think they have failed us. It works, but at what cost! You can probably remember thinking, "All right, if you think I'm no good for anything, then I'll *be* no good!" Or you may sometimes suspect that your parents want you to fail, so that you will continue to need them; but even if this is so, what a waste of yourself it is to try to follow such direction! Even the most loving parent may hate to see his child grow up, since it is daily proof that he will one day be left alone. It is no surprise that a parent will occasionally want his "baby" back. In later life, every adult yearns, too, to return to the old relationship, and wants to be "mothered" or "fathered" on occasion, in order to regain a sense of security.

Feelings of security come when our parents have a generous definition of what "love" means. It is not always having someone close to you, dependent upon you or you dependent on them. Instead, loving means being able to encourage growth and independence and taking pleasure in seeing this happen. Saint-Exupéry's definition of love as, not looking at one another, but "looking together in the same direction" says it well. Insecurity, like most of our self-evaluative feelings, is inherited, not through the genes, but through the feelings of our parents. If they are unsure of themselves—and we do not learn this sometimes until our late teens—they will pass it on to us. Their fears about the world, life, and how they will be treated will create in us an apprehensiveness which we cannot pin down to anything specific. Because we always think that our parents are the wisest, strongest, most important people in the world, it seems that there must be some immense, indefinable terror loose in the world to be able to shake them. Actually, they are very humanly susceptible to the many small frights and alarms of daily living.

Occasionally, as parents see their life ahead of them as being perilous, or their past as unsatisfactory, they may begin to burden their children with unfulfilled hopes and fears about the future. They emphasize good grades. They say they don't want you to suffer as they did. Their overprotectiveness may confirm your worst fears and create entrenched feelings of timidity. They select all the potential disasters of the world to talk about, until you begin to wonder how anyone ever got through this far. Because of their anxiety that you do well, they may press for achievement beyond your capacity. Thus, continually confronted with not measuring up, you become convinced that this must always be so.

Parents frightened of the future may undermine success and a feeling of security with such remarks as, "See how strong Daddy's little boy is; he'll take care of him when he's old, won't he?" With sufficient repetition of such remarks, very often not intended to be taken literally, a child can get the impression that an inviolable contract has been made, the implications of which are immense.

The tendency to take things literally is present in everyone as an attempt to seek immediate reassurance about the structure of the world. The power of the word as a tool for getting what we want begins at the same time as control of bowel and bladder. The child will attempt to substitute the word for the act. He says he went to the potty when he really wet his pants. Because words can do so much to cause wanted action to occur—Milk! Candy! Water!—we continue to believe in them despite a conscious recognition that they do not always mean what they say.

The attempt to protect himself from feared disapproval causes the child to try to separate off from himself the uncontrolled "bad" side of himself. He will "project" onto others, a brother or sister or an imaginary character like an invisible companion. This is a useful device, since it protects for a moment—the time immediately after a misstep, when tension and confusion are at their highest point—until the event can be put into proper perspective. When the event is properly evaluated, then personal responsibility can be accepted and dealt with. Parents may reinforce this method of dealing with problems. "My Mary didn't do that; she couldn't have, because she's a good girl." When the child bumps into a chair, mother may say, "Did the chair hurt my little boy?—*bad* chair!" It is not surprising that, faced with intolerable tensions, we attempt to reduce the tension to a level we can handle, by whatever means. We must remember that what is tolerable may vary from year to year, and even day to day. Obviously, there are no "bad" chairs when we are well co-ordinated adults; but when suddenly surprised as we stub a toe, we may regress to the "bad chair" concept and kick it with our other foot.

The Period of Early Sexual Development

During this time, children show their first interest in sexual differences. A boy at three or four will ask why girls don't have a penis. Told that boys and girls are born different, he may go on to disclose a further interest in what the difference is. He may not completely understand the answer, but he will understand whether or not he has gotten the go-ahead sign to ask again when the worry arises as to why a girl doesn't possess a penis.

A four-year old girl watching her year-old brother getting bathed asked, "Will I grow one when I grow up?" She revealed a sense of discontent with the state of things that could be resolved best by an assurance that she is loved as she is. The acceptance of difference when we feel unsure of ourselves is always difficult.

These very same questions will rearise later in more detail as we grow and need to expand our knowledge of the interrelatedness of new facts, such as pregnancy or the pleasure of masturbation. Very often parents will have avoided seeing the masturbation of young children and yet have conveyed their negative feelings, so that the child later tries to keep this normal aspect of his sexual development out of his own awareness.

Around age four, children begin to take an added interest in the parent of the opposite sex. Now boys begin to take a proprietary attitude toward mother, and even resent father's presence. Girls lessen their attachment to mother and turn to father for more love and attention. It is natural in any choosing-upsides arrangement like this that there may be some hurt feelings. If the parents can meet this divided loyalty situation with tolerance and good humor, all goes well. But going well for the parents does not mean that the children will escape repercussions. Wanting an exclusive claim upon the affections of the favored parent, they believe that the strength of their wish will be met by an equally strong retaliation. They do not know that a parent's need for exclusiveness in a relationship is not so great as their own. At this time, children begin to dream of "bogeymen" or "witches" who threaten them with harm. These dreams give them a chance to relate their fears to their parents and receive reassurance about their parents' continued love. The little girl can ask Mommy if there really are such things as witches, and mother can tell her no, that she doesn't have to be afraid. Later on she will discover how pretending to be a witch herself will also reassure her that even witches don't have to be witches all the time.

Playing out the role of a person from whom one expects hurt

is a good way to test, in ourselves, the ability of others to control angry, destructive, or hurt feelings. Before we go in to ask the boss for a raise, we may find it useful to actually rehearse aloud first what we will say, and what he may say in response. If we can feel that we can be reasonable to our own proposals, then we suspect that others can be as well. If we have met with rejection, rebuff, and ridicule from our parents in our early attempts to play out roles, we will surely have less confidence in approaching new situations. For instance, good humor may lapse into a threatening teasing. Father may say to his son, "All right, if you don't want me around, I'll go away and never come back, and you'll have to go out and work for your mother." The boy is sure to be frightened. A lifelong attitude that he could never be capable of supporting a woman could result. Continuing attitudes emphasizing incapacity, rather than gradually developing strength and skill, limit the development of self-confidence.

Toward the end of the sixth year, children turn again to the parent of the same sex. They identify with and learn how to become a man like father and marry a woman like mother, and to become a woman like mother and marry a man like father.

Even though there may be things about their parents they don't like and don't want to imitate, it will take a major effort of will to be different. The tendency to love and respect our parents, just because they are our parents, can overcome the effect of considerable friction. Met with a fair amount of mutual respect, the child is sure to rely upon what he sees and hears parents do, and to do likewise. As he sees that he can in fact control himself in new and different ways, he will become more daring in his relations with others.

If the family had another baby after him, he had an early test of his ability to share. He was certain to feel deposed from his favored position, and he had to resolve this feeling somehow. Every parent has had to protect a younger child from the direct expression of aggression of the older. The ability to share must be learned from parents. It is hard to share until the concept that sharing can bring a return of good will is established. Even more difficult to learn is the concept that ability to share can bring a sense of personal enlargement *without* an outside return. Parents can insure the first by their own behavior, but the second can be based only on an internal acceptance of personal worth. The child who feels that his parents do not value him can grow into the man who works hard to get people's love and affection but then thinks of them as "suckers" because they like him and are willing to show it by doing things for him. He misses the solid satisfaction of his own labors, because he never really believes that others could love him if his parents did not.

THE YEARS BETWEEN SEVEN AND THIRTEEN

Moving into an enlarged area of activity and relationships always brings new anxiety. The child who has learned to deal with his parents must now learn to deal with his peers. People our own age are not always so kind as our elders. When he goes to school the teacher may be accepting, but he has to prove himself to his schoolmates. If he brings into this new situation an insecurity that is greater than he can see in others, he may be frightened and withdraw.

The last child of a family of seven felt that after he became six everyone else grew up but he didn't. Even kids his own age looked like "big people" to him. He didn't talk to anyone he didn't absolutely have to. At nineteen, on Guadalcanal with the 1st Marine Division, under attack from Japanese battleships and bombers, he felt free for the first time in his life. He saw that other people were afraid too. He went through the entire Pacific Campaign always afraid, but reassured and able to bear it better than others, because he now saw that he was not alone in his fear.

When a person approaches problems by looking into himself and his feelings, thinking first of altering something in his perception of the problem, he may be said to be *introverted*. If, instead, he looks to others about him and works with their reactions as a means of evaluating a problem, he may be said to be an *extrovert*. Both approaches have their advantages. Whether we will use one or the other depends upon our experience in our earlier development.

The introvert may have found that he could gain his parents' approval best by withdrawing and thinking about a problem and working it out in his own mind. He has moved from "playing out" problems to constructing images in his mind. He uses daydreaming and fantasy to practice meeting situations which he considers dangerous to his security. Everyone uses this to some degree, since it enables us to test a situation in our minds with very little expenditure of energy. The extrovert still prefers to play out the solution to his problems on the stage of life. He may regard fantasy only as the briefest necessary period which will show him where he might go. After that, he'll play it by ear. There is a sense of immediate response which can be gratifying if the response is an approving one.

In these years between seven and thirteen, different approaches to being accepted by both adults and peers are tried. Yet much time is spent in a reworking of attitudes toward self and others that were given approval by our parents.

If an older brother or sister has "staked out a claim" on the role of the good student, we may find it difficult to compete. It may seem that there is no approval left to be gained in that area, and some individuals look for another claim to be mined. Even if our parents seem to be interested in our doing well in school, we would rather try something new. One thing is sure: we can act as though we don't care about school. Some of us are bright enough to act as though we don't care, yet be able to do well enough with little study to more than just get by. Or we might be "the musical one" and let something else go. If we depend more heavily upon the approval of our peers than upon that of our parents, we may even take up the role of "the stupid one" or "the delinquent" in order to be popular.

We can give up trying for approval from our age group and act as though we don't care. "They don't matter to me," we rationalize, and we'll "show them" by getting better grades. Thus someone whose parents are little interested in grades becomes a person who aggressively utilizes his intellect to achieve a sense of security.

Latency

This word is used to describe the fact that from age seven to puberty sexual development, though not visible or apparent, is still not dormant. There is, however, an emphasis upon testing and retesting in the development of relationships and the skills that make them easier. Unless curiosity has been blunted, each fact of our existence is continually re-evaluated in the new setting of our continued growth. This growth itself makes old facts new.

Friends to share our ideas and feelings are most important as we come nearer the teen years. The boys pal together doing "masculine" things, and the girls do the same learning to be feminine. Because each attempt at friendship at this age means facing possible rejection, new relations are considered carefully and approached gingerly. Being like the gang is as important now as it is in adolescent and adult behavior, when we go "beat" or get into an Ivy League suit, or follow the changes in fashion and make-up.

"Best friends" can be a pretty closed system, and while it offers a good deal of security, its breakup may lead to reluctance to try again. One or both parties may remain isolated for a fairly long time unless someone helps them out of it. During these isolated periods, we are often evaluating the sense of depression and its boundaries, really seeing how far this feeling will go. It is the rare child who hasn't said, "I wish I were dead," sometimes adding, "Then they'd see!" when it is someone other than himself who has caused his depressed feelings. Most often we want to work it out ourselves and are careful not to let someone kid us out of it ("Be careful now, you might smile!") before we are ready.

When we feel alone and not filled with friendship or security (and no one can all the time, especially at this age), we may give in to the impulse to steal things, often practically valueless objects, as in all the great five-and-dime thefts that Woolworth's has suffered over the years. Such obviously disapproved-of behavior may be used to prove to ourselves that, after all, the adults in the world cannot really read our minds.

Many a child's first experience with outside authority has occurred in the dime store, at the corner grocery, or in the principal's office. Sometimes this petty pilfering is secretly regarded as "cute" by the parents, in which case there is liable to be more until it can no longer be regarded so lightly. Sometimes a parent can preach one thing and practice another. An eight-year old boy stole a rubber stamp set from a dime store. When his mother found it, she lectured him at length about the viciousness of stealing and said she was going to return it. When the boy later found it, used, in his mother's desk drawer, his disappointment in her was crushing.

Some parents, in an attempt to get their children to accept authority outside the home, will almost abandon their parental responsibility to view with reasonable criticalness the contemplated corrective measures of authority. Since no one likes to feel abandoned, even when in the wrong, only lifelong resentment toward authority can result. When stopped for speeding or given a ticket by a police officer for parking too long, even when we are totally in the wrong, we tend to feel a sense of personal injury. We do not often see this injury as it is: self-inflicted. Instead, we think of all the reasons why no police officer should ever give a ticket to anyone as upright and just as we are. We tend to deny the fact of our own violation of the law by returning to the childhood cry of "I didn't do anything!"

Lying successfully is one of the early challenges to our belief that our parents are all-knowing. It is an important discovery, but one we are suspicious about all our lives. We will flock to listen to a magician tell us about ourselves when he has no apparent way of knowing about us. We lie when we are afraid, not only of punishment but of destroying someone else's image of themselves, of us, or of life.

Parents can intensify the child's normal impulse to lie as a means of feeling separate and independent by excessive threats and by lying behavior themselves. "I can always tell when you are lying!" is usually a lie itself.

A child of seven was playing around a fire, and his father could smell the smoke in his clothes when he came home. Father asked, "Were you playing around a fire?"—which was an essentially unfair question, since he could have presented the evidence to encourage telling the truth. The boy lied; father said he knew it was a lie, added that both he and God hated a liar, and administered a beating. Twenty years later, the son hated his wife because he knew she was a liar. He would ask her if she had smoked a cigarette, a habit of which he disapproved. The wife, trained from childhood herself to lie to avoid disapproval, said "No." But he could smell the smoke!

How much more likely people would be to tell the truth where it is appropriate if they were not frightened. It would seem better if we were taught *how* people who are better at seeing things than we are when we are young can guess what we have done. Not "Johnny! Have you been in the cookie jar?" But "Johnny, I can see the cookie crumbs on your face and I don't need to ask you if you've been in the cookie jar. I don't want you to eat those cookies until you've asked." No magic here! Perhaps we don't have to be pushed or trapped into lying in order to learn that truth is valuable.

Puberty

This is the designation for the period at which sexual maturity is reached, and it seems to occur just about the time we begin to feel some stability. We thought we had settled the boy-girl problem in favor of liking our own sex, but now begin hormonal changes that make us change our minds. Because so many things seemed settled, we may be reluctant to begin again the search for a new stability. If we were wise, we might decide now that change is more constant than anything else in life!

Once again the neat sections into which we fitted people and things become all run together like a melted honeycomb. People who were relatively indifferent now look longingly at each other and wonder if they ever can be friends. The physical evidences of the inner hormonal changes that mean biological adulthood proceed at their own set pace. Developing breasts and widening hips are seen in girls, while deepening voices, increased height, broadening shoulders, and heavier muscle structure are seen in boys. Girls show these signs of maturity earlier than boys by about a year. Girls tend to treat boys their own age disdainfully, and their interest and attention go to the boys who are a year or two older and who are ready to return it.

We no longer have to make up secrets as we did in the past, for there are real secrets now. "She's under the moon," "she's fallen off the roof," "she has her period," are cabalistic statements heard about menstruation, a normal development of womanhood. Sometimes such phrases as "she's sick," or "she has the curse" betray our reluctance to accept this new sexual maturation. Boys are concerned about the seminal fluid released at the height of sexual feelings. "Wet dreams" are a source of embarrassment. As boys talk this over, ideas about depletion and loss of strength are expressed, but it is soon found that these are untrue.

It is easy to be out of step through no fault of your own. If your physical development parallels that of most of the group around you, you have the support of knowing that it is happening to everyone. Today it is easier to feel this support than it was in the past when the bodily changes of puberty and early adolescence were taboo subjects. Still, we feel our own internal resistance to this change and the added emotional work that it requires. This is often projected upon a perfectly adequate body in the form of worries about too soon, too late, too little, too much.

Now we must learn and be something new, and this new development often brings with it a feeling of presumption. Our parents who loved us as infants and children must now accept us as early adults. Will they? Can they tolerate this new emergence, our demands for self-determination? Are we insurrectionists against or inheritors of all they have done before us? Our biologic impatience with things as they are is mirrored in our psychologic wish for independence. We may remind those about us that we are in "a world we never made."

APPROACH TO ADULTHOOD (AGES 13 TO 20)

Early adolescence is concerned with looking critically at ourselves and those around us for signs of acceptance. Even the slightest rebuffs can convince us that there is no place for us in the world. Signs of acceptance and love can carry us to the peaks of elation. We need to explore the dimensions of our feeling. We go "way out" and "way in." This exploration has to suffer the constraint of being bound by what really is, but it is often unnecessarily hampered by distorted ideas of what people *should* think and *should* feel.

Like Ulysses, we are a part of all that we have met. Even as adults, we can experience anew the indignity of that early period of learning to control our excretory functions, for the hospital bedpan can remind us of our unwillingness to make public what we were painfully taught to regard as a private function. We do not even want to share it with the nurse. We were also taught that our sexual functions were likewise private. Many people equate the two, calling them both dirty. Kipling's lines reveal our continued conflict over self-discipline:

> Ship me somewhere east of Suez
> Where the best is like the worst
> Where there ain't no Ten Commandments
> And a man can raise a thirst.

Perhaps we seek some place where anything we might do would be all right.

Each older generation fears the strength of the sexual drives of the younger in proportion to the often unremembered struggle they went through to control their own impulses. The usual technique of control is fear. The military services show films on the perils of venereal diseases. Parents warn against the dangers of "touching yourself." Although fear is seen as a short-cut to control, fear itself can be a stimulus to masturbation. We have to conceal even the minor evidence of our sexual interests which we feel are so bad, and fall back on ourselves. The older generation often forgets its own experimentation. There seems to be a distrust of reasonableness, of explanation, and of trust. Because masturbation and sexual feelings are inevitable, we have a built-in reason for distrusting ourselves. We naturally think, if we cannot completely control ourselves, that we are liable to lose control at any instant. This applies not only to sexual but to aggressive impulses and thoughts as well. If we could believe our own experience and would look around us at other people and their behavior, we would know that this is not necessarily true.

We attempt many different diversions to keep these tensions at a low level. We try to separate the thought and the feeling. Testing ourselves, we think about or get into sexual situations and then repress any sexual feelings. A subculture can develop around "coolness" in essentially hot situations. We reverse it: perceiving the sexual feeling, we block any sensuous thoughts, although thereby actually increasing the intensity of them. This attitude is a basic defense of the "beat generation," which pretends to itself to be influenced by its own impulses.

We may try to interchange fear of one thing with fear of another. Instead of being afraid of our real thoughts and feelings, we are afraid of open or closed spaces, elevators, bridges, heights, basements, birds, insects, and so on. We can *really* keep away from all these things. We also attempt to keep disturbing thoughts out of our minds by filling them with repetitious ideas, that recur over and over. Silly things, songs, melodies, numbers, frightening things, anything but the thoughts we are afraid to admit. We develop little reassuring rituals, like the familiar knocking on wood or throwing salt over the shoulder, and many that are private.

We have all felt the urge to resolve the struggle of these basic instincts either by giving in to all of them that people around us would permit, or by trying to disavow them altogether. Asceticism and self-denial seem attractive recourses when things get to be "just too much."

Moodiness is particularly pronounced during adolescence. Everyone has experienced ups and downs in mood, feeling good at one time and bad at another. If you are busy doing something, you might not even notice your mood. You have had the experience of hearing someone around you say, "Well, aren't we happy today!" when you are unaware of the fact that you were whistling happily or walking jauntily. You have also noticed that when people ask, "What are you frowning about?" you find that sadness was in the back of your mind.

In both instances, some activity or concentration upon something outside yourself serves to disguise or conceal your mood from yourself. It can even help us forget pain. We have all had the experience of being hurt and going to the movies, where we were caught up in the story and then "forgot" our pain. Hypnosis, too, is a voluntary effort and agreement to concentrate our interest so that we can disregard sensations in ourselves and distraction from the outside. This can be done so well that many ordinarily painful things, like the dentist filling a tooth, can be done without "feeling" the pain. Actually we neither forget nor escape feeling the pain; we simply do not pay attention to it.

This may be useful, since it teaches us that being active or being interested in something outside of ourselves can work to make us more cheerful or more sober. You know from this that you can actively take a hand in changing your mood. Some timid or frightened people, responding to changing life situations, may actually adopt one prevailing mood, most often unknowingly but sometimes consciously. They are *pessimists,* grouches, always singing the blues. Their solution to meeting the ever changing problems of living is to avoid committing themselves beyond a very low level of expectation. Of course, this may be a façade behind which a person attempts to conceal a very active interest in life. He feels that if he exposed it, others would think him a pollyanna or a fool. He would say, "An optimist is someone who puts off suicide for just one more day."

The *optimist* may attempt, much more pleasantly for those around him, always to see things in their brightest light. Little Mary Sunshine's smile may occasionally get a little strained around the jaw, but because the attitude you bring with you in your attempt to solve problems has a great effect upon what happens, a positive view will most often carry the day. Even this has its danger, because it is a single approach. The paraphrase of Kipling's "If" gives a pessimist's appreciation of this fact. "If you can keep your head when all about you are losing theirs—then you just don't understand the situation." Because an optimistic view can include the ability to let go of past defeats and failures, it frees energy and thought for present and future problems.

If people around you describe you as consistently depressed, suspicious, guilty, angry, or whatever, pay attention. You may unknowingly have developed a mood or attitude to protect you from your fears, but one which also prevents you from responding appropriately to life.

When Betty went out on dates, she was always a little apprehensive about how she would be liked. Though she was attractive, other girls seemed to be more successful in having their dates ask to see them again. She wondered why. What was the problem? Becauses she was so apprehensive, she played the clown, making a caricature of the warm friendly self she wanted to be. She giggled and postured, responding more to her own fear than to her date. Even after this was called to her attention and she recognized what was happening, she had difficulty changing. After all, she was still apprehensive. As she learned that she could voluntarily focus her interest on her date and away from herself, she began to act more poised and secure. This increased her sense of self-esteem, so that it was less necessary for her to protect herself by acting the clown.

Here, being more sober and calm was important, but what about feeling depressed and down in the mouth? These feelings may be reactions to events in our daily lives. Parting from people we love, leaving places where we were happy, or losing things that were mementos or keepsakes, symbols of the fondly remembered past, are sure to result in our feeling sad. After such losses, we mourn for a time. We are reluctant to give up what is gone and to seek new relationships to take their place. We even feel a little angry at what is gone for having left us, as though by leaving, it willfully took this feeling of closeness away from us. When a friend does willfully leave us, we often feel only anger at first. Later we may wonder what we did to make him go. We may berate ourselves because of what we did or did not do to keep a friend. We can see that, after all, it was not our friend, but what we did, and so the anger we first felt against him is turned back on ourself. This, added to our sense of loss, can make our depression even deeper. Even if we have done nothing, we always think a little that we must in some way be responsible.

John was only seven when he wished his abusive alcoholic

father would die, and the father did die. He died of a heart attack, yet John was convinced that his wish had done it. He felt a great sense of guilt, even when he was 27 years old and a medical student, and knew that it could not have been his fault.

We can see this tendency to believe that we did something wrong in the case of adopted children who feel that they must get to know their real parents. They want to find out what happened. This pressure is felt even after long years of love and pleasure in the relationship with the foster parents.

How can you understand these daily fluctuations in mood which you feel? In order to function in the world, we must constantly create images and construct ideas. These images and ideas, sometimes called fantasies, help us to see our place in the order of things. We begin early in life to "make believe." We play at being aviator, fireman, Indian chief, mother, father, and a host of other things. As we grow older, we no longer play these things out, but instead think them out in daydreams. These are useful, because with very little expenditure of energy we can explore wide areas of possibility. We can be the first man to land on Mars. We can be a master of men and of ourself. We can dream of danger and practice how to meet it. The usefulness of such an approach to problem-solving is demonstrated in "blue sky" sessions of research teams, where each participant is asked to contribute ideas, no matter how wild or how much they do violence to current concepts.

Of course, because it is easy, daydreaming can become an end in itself rather than a preparation for more controlled and directed thinking and planning for future action. Then it becomes enervating and discouraging.

Because we live in a real world, each fantasy is eventually tested against the possibility of accomplishment. At such times, it is inevitable that part of the fantasy is destroyed and lost. Sometimes people cannot bear to give up a thought in which they have invested a great deal of emotion, and they try to defy or ignore the real world.

Mary stands at the window of her hospital room watching for her fiancé, who is going to come today and pick her up. At any minute she expects to see him drive up. She has been expecting him every day for six months, despite the fact that they broke their engagement two years ago. While this adherence to an idea is far in excess of what we usually find, there are ideas which we hold to just as desperately, even if we are not confronted with such overwhelming evidence against them.

Thus in the history of medicine, there was strong resistance to the existence of microbes, which live everywhere around us. It was difficult to believe that things that we could not see or touch could make us sick. In order to avoid the hard work involved in rearranging their thinking, many men fought against this idea. Some must have been quite depressed, or even preferred to ignore this new information completely. Yet those who accepted the concept, even before it was definitely proved true by Pasteur, must have experienced the joy and elation that come with having our beliefs confirmed. Such an experience is like having the world and life itself accept you, along with your accepting the world.

To a small degree these emotions are stirred in you each day. As you dream, fantasize, construct an idea, think, and do, you are each day having the experience of losing part of the whole and of having part of it confirmed. The degree of depression or elation you feel will depend upon the amount of emotion you have invested. If little, you can give it up or have it confirmed with relative indifference; if much, then with proportionate regret or pleasure.

All of these gambits and diversions are normal way stations on the road to acceptance of ourselves, society, and the place we can make for ourselves in it.

People are fond of quoting Mark Twain as saying, "When I was fourteen I thought my father was awful dumb, but when I was twenty-one, I was surprised to find out how much the old man had learned in seven years." The teen-ager who once thought his parents were perfect now begins to criticize them. Not, as parents often think, because he is ungrateful, unappreciative, or unloving, but because he is so critical of himself. Everything connected with himself comes in for the same searing examination: father, mother, brother, sister, teacher, school, clothes, and so on. If parents take this personally, they may fight to suppress this process. Even their rare reminders of past support are resented. We need *ourselves* to accept the appropriateness of our criticism of our parents, for surely there will be some that is appropriate. This is hard for us to do, because our parents are so much a part of ourselves that we would rather fight about them in the hope that we can be overcome and return to the idea of their perfection. If we are fortunate, our parents will use our appropriate criticisms as an opportunity to demonstrate the value of self-acceptance. Deficiencies need to be tolerated, and if parents can tolerate their own when pointed out by their children, the children can learn, by example, to tolerate the gross imperfections they find in themselves. If this doesn't happen, these teen-agers grow into nagging wives and husbands. Anyone who could love them *must* be inferior. Because they feel they themselves are not good enough, anything that belongs to them is thought of in the same way. They try to improve themselves by improving others.

A young girl of a family of moderate means was always criticizing her mother. She herself felt left out of the crowd at school, lonely and unappreciated. It was painful to take this rejection into herself. Her mother did, indeed, have many deficiencies. Some thirty years later, the daughter remembered with a wince that her mother had said to her, "You won't be satisfied with me until I'm the Duchess of Windsor." She had felt so lonely herself that she was really asking her mother to be an entirely different person; someone grand in whose shadow she could stand.

Most of us can recall having the thought that our parents were not our real parents, but only substitutes for famous, powerful people who could help us out of our shy loneliness just by being.

Our inappropriate criticism can be understood as part of the excessive self-examining process of adolescence. Yet every parent might remember that in our socially striving society, he may well be outside the mainstream of what is considered "correct" behavior. Their willingness to learn brightens the self-assurance of their children immensely.

Adolescence

What are the major problems facing the adolescent?

The first is becoming independent not only of his parents but also of his own impulses so that he can work at recognizing and accepting himself and others for what they are. With appreciation of self comes freedom to accept and appreciate others for what is positive in them with less need to emphasize their faults. Too often we confuse independence with license. We forget that rules are not blocks to progress, although occasionally they can be; if they all seem so, we have to face the fact that we are surely wrong. Most of us are too smart to confront ourselves with such overwhelming evidence of irresponsibility. If instead we can convince ourselves that it's just this rule today and another the next that we object to, we may continue to dodge responsibility while pretending to ourselves that we want to be, and are, independent.

Pete said he didn't object to everything his parents asked him to do. It was just that he didn't want to take out the trash today. Then later he didn't want to put up the screens. Saturday he didn't want to come home before one A.M. When he worked he didn't like to get up in the morning. Paydays, he didn't want to contribute his share to the house; later he'd "borrow" it back. He didn't want to return it. He got his parents to push him even to do things for himself. He thought he was independent when he left home on a scholarship to an upstate college. In a year he was back—there had been no one to force him to study.

We want independence but forget that it is something that has to be practiced to become part of us. We often encourage our parents to withhold it. To balk at simple everyday rules of behavior may fool some people around us into believing that we are independent characters, but only the most naive are taken in. Ordinary rules of behavior are the grease of life. They reduce the friction of interpersonal relationships and make things go smoothly. So to be independent, we must take up the task of responsible behavior whenever it is appropriate to our skill. This does not mean that we should not rely upon others. We can and indeed should, if we are ourselves appropriately active in our own and others' interest.

The second major problem is forming heterosexual relationships. While we all have to have enough feeling for members of our own sex to enable us to work, play, think, and feel together, we need to be able to develop a more intense and physical relationship with the opposite sex.

The French may exclaim, "Vive la différence!" in the matter of the sexes, but the difference causes anxiety in the adolescent. Although this anxiety is not easily relieved, it does gradually diminish when getting together is recognized as a mutual desire.

If the individual thinks his interest is intrusive, he will continue to expect rebuff. Then more than ever he will be afraid of the difference. In order not to feel rebuff as a personal thing (after all, mating is a matter of selecting and choosing sides), men have for centuries remarked upon the inscrutable female mind. It is quite possible that this has been one way of avoiding having to think about women and their needs and desires. Having to think about anything is, of course, hard work. Actually, women are quite understandable. Women have a similar misconception of men: "Why won't men understand," they say. Usually this reflects the fact that they regard their needs for reassurance and love as a burden which men accept only unwillingly. The differences are there, of course, but of far greater importance is the mutual goal. Both have the pattern of their parents before them and will most likely follow it in their attempts to get close to each other.

The "will she, won't she, will he, won't he" preoccupation of popular songs would be better replaced by "how can I help make happen in my own case the natural coming together of the sexes?" The capacity to convey respect for the feelings, even the anxieties of others, is most important. Advice that can cover all situations is hard to come by, but one of the first principles of medicine can be applied:

Primum non nocere.
(Above all, do no harm.)

Jerome K. Jerome humorously remarked, long before Dale Carnegie, "Fill a man (or woman) with love for himself and what runs over will be your share." But if someone has not laid a foundation, this can be an endless task. Oftentimes it seems that parents and society in general try hard to prevent people from getting together. But since the responsibilities of marriage are considerable, making haste slowly is well advised. It is, of course, good advice only for those who *can* make haste. The problems of meeting and "getting to know you" are met by institutions designed to help while still protecting. Parties, games, dances, social affairs, activities of all kinds that will bring people together in patterned relationships help. For each activity you need to learn the ground rules. These give the directions almost as clearly as the stage directions for a play. The need for such direction all our lives is reflected in the continued use of such books as the enlisted men's or officers' guide in the services and Emily Post's book about etiquette. While these things often seem, and occasionally are, foolish, they serve to smooth the way to easier relationships. Because all societies, like individuals, are in constant change, the rules change too and so must the rule books. What appears to be fact and useful as a guide for behavior today may be no longer true tomorrow.

John was always encouraged to study and do well in school. His mother, herself born to difficult times in Europe, praised him for not being "girl crazy" and for being serious-minded. "What's in your mind you won't have to pack on your back," she'd say. Then one day she heard that the other boys in the neighborhood were going to a dance and she asked John why he didn't go too. He was furious. "For 18 years you've been telling me not to pay attention to girls—now you ask me why I'm not going to the dance! Because I can't dance—that's why!" Mother didn't know this. But John knew and could have done something about it.

Love is difficult to define. It encompasses the idea of working for a common goal—the freely given and acted-upon wish for the growth, security, independence, and happiness to the limit of his potential of another human being.

The first requirement of loving is to be loved yourself. The people around you when you were small gave you whatever start you had. If they were afraid that you'd be spoiled by a good opinion of yourself, your start toward loving others was a lame one at best. Little by little you have to find new sources of love, the most important of which is yourself. The creative use of your own capacities enables you to love yourself. Many people mistake this for selfishness, but only those people who love themselves can truly love others. If you reject self-love, you are rejecting your own wish for your growth, security, independence, and happiness. If you cannot allow yourself the freedom to want these things for yourself, you will be poor company for anyone else.

If you are always carping because of what you are not, you cannot love. You must make a realistic assessment of yourself that is generous as well as critical and then work with what you have.

As you think about marriage you will remember your parents' relationship and sort out the good from the bad. If you have not permitted yourself the honesty to recognize the good and bad in your parents' marriage, you will probably make the same mistakes and enjoy about the same pleasures. The most outstanding fact about marriage is that it gives you the chance to know another person intimately. The opportunity is there; whether you use it or not depends on you. You came from different backgrounds, no matter how similar. Some ideas you share and some you will find difficult to understand. If you are willing to work at understanding without turning every request to be understood into an accusation against which you must defend yourself, most differences can be worked out.

If we are unwise, we work out our old resentments toward our parents or friends in our marriage. We can make our wives into mothers who are to scold us, and our husbands into fathers who are distant and never understand.

Robert married a soft, feminine, uncomplaining, giving girl who tried to please him. But something was stuck in his craw. He couldn't be himself. He was used to being scolded and feeling put upon in his relations with women. Although he sincerely wished this were not so, in spite of himself he began a campaign that turned his wife into a source of irritation. He wouldn't use an alarm clock, so his wife had to wake them. He would then get ugly, using early morning grouchiness as an excuse. He pretended she was unreasonable when she wanted to go out, always acting as though he would not accompany her until the last minute. Then he would say, "You didn't really think I'd let you go without me, did you?" He even went so far as to train her not to have intercourse with him, so that he could complain and feel unloved and mistreated. At last he was at home.

Jane seemed a better picker than Robert at first. She married a reserved man who relied upon intellect and logic to deal with problems. This went fine at work, but at home Jane began to complain that he couldn't understand the finer things in life (meaning herself principally). She would come home from an art exhibit or lecture and start to tell her husband about it, then stop and say, "Oh, you wouldn't understand—you don't understand the subjective or emotional." He tried on many occasions to show that he was willing to learn, but Jane would have none of it. He finally showed her he had emotion enough even if he didn't understand it. He divorced her.

MATURITY AND MENTAL HEALTH

What will we do when we "grow up"? Everyone faces a decision with some basic insecurity, especially when the decision eliminates other possible courses of action. Because of this, many of us put off decisions as long as we can in order to fool ourselves into thinking that so long as we do not decide, all possibilities are open before us.

What is maturity but responsibility taken with a good heart? To work; to be friendly and confident in relations with others; to love, in the conventional heterosexual way, and also to love the neighborhood, state, nation, and world; to pass on to others what you have learned. Mental health is the capacity to look at life with tolerance, humor, and curiosity. We are endowed biologically with an amazing mechanism, our brain. From the day we were born, and before, it has been scanning, sorting, and storing perceptions and information. It can give us the sum and feel of an experience in a moment. If this sum and feel is unpleasant, it can distort it just enough so that it doesn't hurt so much. When comfort and memory are in conflict, memory tends to give way.

As we grow and mature, we have hundreds of little problems to solve and each one seems major, because it is worked at as separate and distinct from all the others. Gradually, as each of them is resolved, we forget the effort that went into their solution. None of us can recall the effort of learning to balance ourselves in order to walk. If we twist an ankle or a knee or have to wear glasses, we face again the major rearrangement that even small physical changes require. The same applies to emotional problems.

It is both harder and easier to make changes later in life. It is harder because the way we deal with problems has become relatively fixed into patterns and because we usually have the responsibility of dealing with more than one problem at a time. Going into a hospital, for instance, is a way to relieve ourselves of multiple responsibilities in order to focus our problem-solving abilities on getting well. It is easier to make changes in later life because we recognize problems as similar to others we have solved in the past. Grouping problems according to this similarity carries the danger, however, that we will put the problem in the wrong category. Once we do this, there is a reluctance to change it or to see the problem differently.

A mother and teen-age daughter came to a psychiatric clinic to complain about each other, the mother about her daughter's refusal to abide by rules, and the daughter about mother's total inability to be a mother. They agreed that they were poles apart and could never get together. Yet as mother talked, she constantly watched her daughter's pouting out of the corner of her eye, so that her reactions to her daughter rather than the sense of what she was saying punctuated her sentences. The daughter talked to the doctor but always looked at her mother. They had worked long and hard at their problem of getting along together but they had categorized their problem incorrectly. They were not poles apart as they thought—they were too close together.

Handling Anger

Many people discover early in life the release of tension and blunting of fear that a feeling of anger can give. The earliest response of the naturally insecure, frustrated infant to what is new or different is anger. In the same way, the first response of the insecure, frustrated adult is anger. Behind both lie only desperation or desperate action. So long as the feeling of anger is maintained, most anxiety is submerged. Anger may not be enough to subdue our fear, and we go further and become enraged. By these means we escape the need for finer judgments about any situation. We abandon reasonableness in an attempt to gain a feeling of ungoverned power. The goal is to "drown out" the apprehension that frustration brings.

You can go through life with a low boiling point as a method of dealing with problems, but you will not be liked. As with dictators, most people will avoid the challenge of your anger or rage around small matters, but you can never know when they will take up the challenge and fight against you. Or they can simply, by baiting you repeatedly, stimulate your insecurity and exhaust your defenses by causing you to strike out at shadows. If you can recognize the natural tendency to use anger to avoid fear, you can separate it from anger that is more appropriate to damage done or threatened, and take active steps to prevent its recurrence.

Handling Prejudice

It seems appropriate to discuss prejudice next, because it is a way of expressing our anger in concert with others, utilizing group agreement to reinforce an unsupportable argument. We carefully avoid contradictory evidence or throw the emotion of anger into the breech if we become too threatened.

Why does prejudice exist? Why do people hold themselves back from a close examination of the new or different? One answer that is not malignant is economy. A cowboy who had always lived a rather Spartan life, empty of small luxuries, visited some friends in a small town. He was reluctant to try new foods or accept little courtesies from his friends. They thought he must be embarrassed and just needed encouraging. So one morning when they were serving bananas with the cereal, they insisted that he try some. No, he refused, he'd never had bananas before. Well, they said, he should try some as he might like them. "That's just it," he said. "I've already got more tastes than I can satisfy."

This approach to new experiences guarantees a simplicity that makes life easier to manage, but also makes it somewhat barren.

Some people fear new relations with people because they do not feel they can give enough of themselves to interest someone else. Or they are afraid that, even if they could, they would leave themselves emotionally bankrupt. It is easy, then, for such people to fall into the pattern of explaining their fear of relations with others on the basis of concepts of prejudice.

"Miriam thinks she is so good looking. She's stuck-up. All these flashy, good-looking girls are no good."

If Miriam is Catholic, Jewish, Protestant, or Negro, or can be fitted into any larger category, we can hide from ourselves and deny the fear that we will not be interesting enough to her or be accepted by her. We can explain our "sour grapes" attitude by saying *she* is no good, and bolster this attitude and conceal its basis in our own fear by saying that everyone like her is no good.

Once we begin using this pattern of self-deception, it becomes easy to transfer it to many problems that we face. On the job, for instance, when someone is promoted ahead of us, we can say he belongs to the class of apple-polishers. He does not have real merit; he just says nice things to others.

Some girls start out feeling that to use make-up, like others their age, or to dress in the current style is superficial and a little degrading. They feel it is not honest. Actually, this is a way that society has evolved of signaling, "I like myself and I want you to like me." These signals are incorporated in how we dress and use make-up, perfume, and accessories. Although we complain about the frequent changes in style that necessitate redoing hemlines or moving a waist up or down, we comply willingly as an index of our interest in self and others. Why don't men's fashions change too? They do. Just look at the demise of ascot ties, wide lapels, broad ties, plus-four trousers. As we have better control of our environment through heating and air conditioning, clothing has more value as a signal of being outgoing than as protection.

To be against changes in style seems a small prejudice, one that we could comfortably indulge, but at its roots are the same insecurities that are present in the more important rejection of ideas and people.

Another answer to why prejudice exists is the utility of prejudice in saving the emotionally bankrupt. When we are feeling afraid and alone, we seek closeness and comfort from others. At such times we are especially vulnerable to developing prejudices. We do not usually think about it, but when we feel insecure or even anticipate insecurity in the future, we can take the easy road of joining people in their hate rather than in their love. In order to join people in their love, we have to *be* something positive ourselves. We can join people in their hate in a state of abject emptiness. We hope that the hating group which we join will overlook *our* deficiencies because we join *them* in sympathy with their hate. Perhaps they will give us the affection and attention we seek and not confirm our feeling of worthlessness. Dictators have said that the creation of an outside enemy is a good strategy to hold together groups of people who might otherwise become restless and discordant, or apathetic. If we want the easy way to acceptance, we can take this way, submerge the sense of uncertainty and challenge which we all feel, and hate.

Intelligence

Intelligence is the ability of our brain to accurately scan, sort, and store perceptions of the sensing organs, such as the eyes, ears, or fingers, as well as internal organs such as the stomach and intestines. In addition, it must be able to co-ordinate these perceptions and make them appropriately available. The facts it reports are our conscious thinking. Those which we can call up easily are "preconscious." Those which operate outside our awareness are "unconscious."

Intelligence tests are a gross measure of the ability of our brain to store perceptions and information, comprehend situations, and solve problems. They are largely measures of thinking abilities which are appropriate to learning in school and functioning on most jobs. It is often thought that a high test score means you can do well at anything and a low score that you can do well at very little. Neither is true on the basis of the test alone. A man might test high on an intelligence examination, while observation shows him to be undirected, inactive, and unimaginative. "What a waste," we say, "with *his* intelligence." Intelligence scores should always be projected upon some background and not accepted by themselves as indices of capacity to achieve. A recent cartoon showed a father talking to his son, who is sprawled before a TV set. Father is saying, "It's not enough to have a high IQ, you have to *do* something!"

Imagination

The most important use of our capacity for thinking is our ability to combine seemingly unrelated and as yet unused events with one another in such a way as to realize new possibilities. This computer that is our brain handles a difficult job in keeping many different experiences and ideas straight. It is not surprising that, when confusion is experienced, it starts re-evaluating *all* the data fed into it, with the result that the most unlikely-seeming things are combined with each other. These new combinations often reinforce patterns that *seemed* likely before, but were not yet studied and clarified, because we were not able to properly sort and group things, people, and situations. We later learned what we could expect of ourselves and what others expected of us and used this information in order to categorize events.

This *ability* of our brain to review all possible correlations between events and things is the most important feature of human existence. Occasionally you will hear someone say that it is the opposed thumb which has differentiated humanity from the other animals. Actually, it is the flexible plasticity of the brain which makes us human. For whatever reason, human beings carry within their skulls the jungle of primitive existence side by side with all the sophistication of civilized living. This capacity to *think anything* and *feel everything* is the single surest guarantee of the continuance of humankind.

Leadership

There are many ways to become a leader. Less and less are people born to lead, and still more rarely is leadership thrust upon them; most have to achieve it. Most college reference forms ask about the leadership ability of the applicant. One daring father wrote of his son that while he was not sure of his leadership ability, he was sure that he was a good and willing follower. Every leader must be a follower of something, usually an idea, a concept of how things or people might be better. Obviously, he could be wrong—and we have many examples of this in recent world events.

Usually our first experience with leadership occurs during that early time when we turn more of our attention to others outside the family. The game "follow-the-leader" is based upon the ability of the leader to make following him seem interesting and challenging. If he does the same old things, the group looks for a new leader. Under pressure, the leader may become daring to the point of foolhardiness. At that point the group must give up following him or risk hurt.

A leader may have discovered (or even pretended to discover) something unknown to the group, and invite others to share it on the condition that they accept his leadership. Leadership may be attained by giving others what they want, a treacherous task at best if one attempts to follow the minute-by-minute fluctuations of what people appear to want. The remark that "a country gets the leaders it deserves" appears to be based on an evaluation of this type of leadership. Satisfying hate, greed, and envy is a dangerous path to leadership. Leaders of this type are most often trying to make up for a lack of love and security in their early life and are willing to pay any price for even a semblance of acceptance. Like everyone who lacks the capacity to appreciate himself, they end with a vehement disregard for the welfare of their adherents.

There are, then, all kinds of leadership possibilities. In our society, the one in great demand is the co-ordinating leader, the man who can bring people together to think and act. He must have the capacity to value the talents of others despite personal prejudices.

What should a leader bring to his task? First, a real degree of competence in which he can feel secure. Second, an acceptance of himself as he is without an undue amount of reservation stemming from early childhood. Third, the willing, unabashed acknowledgement of the limits of his ability. Fourth, readiness to give over leadership in specific areas and become a follower of greater competence. Fifth, a willingness to share not only burdens but successes. Sixth, and most essential, honesty, an honesty that tests itself not only against internal standards of a system of behavior (e.g., "business ethics," dedication to a political, scientific, or artistic movement) but against external standards of moral behavior as well.

Basic to all leadership is the commitment to and discharge of responsibility, whether broadly or narrowly defined. The rewards of leadership are the same as those of parenthood: the pleasure of giving love and seeing the development of strength, security, independence of thought and action, and compassionate understanding.

SUMMARY

The attempt to understand even the simple facts of how we develop is tremendously difficult. Archimedes' statement that if he were given a place to stand and a support for his lever he could move the world, points up the difficulty. There is no place to stand. The observer and the observed are part of the same piece of ground. Only occasionally are we truly able to stand back and look at ourselves and our development. This chapter gives a brief outline of a way of understanding how we become what we are. This concept of our development and how it affects some important attitudes we have toward life presumes a single view of the psychology of man. It conceives of all men as possessing essentially the same drives, aspirations, and conflicts, although these may be muted or accentuated by accidents of birth, environment, and culture.

Becoming the Complete Adult
Spiritually

RELIGIOUS AND
SPIRITUAL
VALUES

by Paul W. Pruyser, Ph.D., Associate Director,
Department of Education at The Menninger
Foundation

and

Karl A. Menninger, M.D., Chairman of the
Board of Trustees of The Menninger Foundation and Chief of Staff of the Menninger Clinic

3

ONE difficulty in talking about values is the fact that the word itself has become so value-laden. It is often used as a shorthand expression for its superlative, greatest value. When we prefix it with such adjectives as religious or spiritual, which also are themselves heavily value-laden, we double or triple the power of the expression. Thus, the title of this chapter, at first sight, suggests an ultimate excellence.

It is our purpose, however, to discuss both value in general and religious and spiritual values in particular, in a broad rather than in a narrow sense. Both a penny and a dollar have value. Both the bicycle thief and the blood donor are behaving morally. The Aztecs offering human sacrifices were exhibiting religious behavior no less than the pious Quakers quietly waiting for the Inner Light.

Ordinarily philosophers, clergymen, and professors of ethics or of economics are the ones from whom we expect essays on value concepts. The present writers are not authorities or philosophers, but they are clinicians. They deal daily with people who are in trouble and want help—or with colleagues who seek instruction and training in the methods of dealing with troubled people. This experience does not equip us to speak comprehensively on the meaning of values, but it does give us a certain slant on the application of the term and the application of the concept.

Ordinarily we clinicians are not supposed to be much concerned with values, and certainly not with those forms of value called religious and spiritual. For doctors generally, the highest value is commonly assumed to be the condition of health. And yet surely every reader knows doctors who highly disapprove of the principles and practices of certain very healthy people. Health is, indeed, considered something of high value by clinicians; it is the value which particularly relates to their professional competence. For a few physicians, perhaps, and for not a few laymen, health has too high a value; but here we are anticipating something.

It is our purpose to discuss values, and particularly religious and spiritual values, in a somewhat systematic and academic way, *from the standpoint* of our own life dedication and clinical orientation.

In philosophical writings, generally a sharp distinction is made between facts and opinions. All scientists are taught to give their primary attention to facts and secondary attention to estimates and interpretations of those facts. It is a question whether value itself is a fact, or only an estimate or "opinion" about facts. For example, that there is such a thing as a diamond is surely a fact. We know that the diamond is hard, that it sparkles, that it can be cut. These are facts. Now can we also say that the diamond has value? Hardness and brilliancy are qualities and their existence is a fact. Is value also a quality or something that can be attributed to the diamond, or is it rather that the state of affairs in human beings is such that they attribute value to the diamond?

The diamond would be hard under all circumstances; but it

will not sparkle under all circumstances. We know, too, that a diamond is very valuable under some circumstances and quite useless under other circumstances—for example, to a hungry Eskimo on a desert island.

It is not our intention to go into an elaborate epistemological study of what is meant by value, but we are obliged to give some considerations to just what the word means before speaking in more general terms. It is obvious that value is different from such qualities as hardness and brilliancy. For while the quality of hardness is the same the world over and whereas brilliancy depends entirely upon light and the reflections of that light, values depend upon the psychological reactions of different human beings in their opinions, beliefs, and expectations. There would be what we call hardness in the world whether there were human beings here to feel it or not, but no values.

As we use the term here we are speaking of value as an estimate, a degree of desirability, a relative importance ascribed to things or acts by someone, or by several someones. This ascription is not a mere verbal one; many people who can talk beautifully about goodness or humanitarianism are very disappointing in the living of these virtues. The distance between "talking" and "doing," as everyone knows, can be considerable. In actual practice, we find evidence in both talk and behavior of an orientation to certain values; one cannot go entirely either by a person's words exclusively or by his deeds exclusively, in order to find out what his values are. There is often some degree of tension between the words and the deeds, the intentions and the acts. Most people could truthfully echo St. Paul's lament: "For the good that I would, I do not; but the evil which I would not, that I do."

CLINICAL DEFINITION OF VALUES

Both verbal utterances (or even the unuttered thoughts) and actual behavior indicative of value estimates are the end products of a complicated system of ideas and forces working in us and upon us. For a practical rule of thumb, one may say that *values are those directive ideas or estimates on the basis of which one is willing to make the greater sacrifices.* This is one way of establishing a measuring rod for a seeming intangible. It uses the pleasure-pain principle as a criterion. Given a variety of opportunities, choices, temptations and stresses, what rule or order of truth and goodness and beauty will a man abide by, even under adverse and difficult conditions, in the face of threat? Given a choice between a serene walk in the woods and a hectic hunting trip, which will a man take? Will an American soldier, captured by Red Chinese, remain loyal to his country's code or will he go to pieces and "confess" to the enemy? Will a wife and mother, upon meeting a new and attractive man who stirs up her romantic girlhood longings, stay faithful to her husband and family, or will she resign from such obligations and undertake a venture regardless of the consequences? The outcome will depend largely upon the values by which one abides.

Since the word value implies a measuring or grading on some kind of a scale, it tends to get used in an appreciative sense— that is, we say value, but we mean the higher value or the highest value. The same thing is true of such words as height; actually height refers only to a perpendicular distance, but we come to use the word height as if it meant great height or length of perpendicular distance.

Similarly, when we talk about values we tend to mean high values, but talking about them in the abstract and living them is of course quite a different matter. Value and choice are thus intimately related to one another. This does not mean, however, that the choices are always conscious, nor that the values are consciously held. Many powerful values are quite unconscious, particularly the negative ones. Take for instance the unreasonable contempt which many people have for members of minority groups. Or take the equally unreasonable disgust which some people have for snakes or cigar smoking or hunting. The radical haters of the rich, the consistent enemies of labor unions, the witch hunters in society, the "commie shouters"—all these are in the grips of strong negative values, mostly held unconsciously. Unaware of the origins and status of these values, they can hardly be engaged in discussion about them.

VALUES ARE ORGANIZED INTO SCALES
OR HIERARCHIES

Values, although maintained as an individual matter, are sustained and often determined by the values held by other people. No two people have quite the same value systems, but many people have similar value systems or value systems that are similar up to a certain point. Since values serve as important guides to behavior, a consistent change and interchange of values in a sense determines history. At one time the Children of Israel felt that it was right and proper and, indeed, godly, to slaughter the inhabitants of the Land of Canaan. For several years, a large number of Germans thought it proper to slaughter Jews. Property rights are so clearly held in mind by most people today that it comes as a shock to realize that at some time or another all land was stolen by somebody from somebody else, and hence that all real estate is "stolen goods." Once a positive value was placed upon owning slaves, later a negative value.

It was long a religious custom to sacrifice the first fruits of life to God, and this included one's own firstborn child. In the same name of religion (though not the same religion) we now hold that this is a horrendous thing. The values placed on God, life, sacrifice, and worship have changed. Within the broad range of Western civilization, the values of men like Nero or Eichmann or Lincoln or Albert Schweitzer are immensely different. Only a hundred years ago, it was quite general that children were drilled into conformity to adult standards regardless of the stifling of their natural tendencies; now we feel that children should have opportunities for spontaneous development of their originality and talents.

But even more important than the dependency of values on culture and historical change is the fact that *every person has within himself a variety of values, some of which may vie with others for priority*. On certain occasions two or more acknowledged values may be incompatible. An example is the story of Jesus confronting the Pharisees about the ox in the ditch on the Sabbath. Can one work on the Lord's day? Adhering to Sabbath laws, the community said no; Jesus gave a qualified yes without devaluating the Sabbath. This was an argument not only about values but more precisely about the rank of several values. The point is that values, which are supposed to be guides for judgments, are themselves judged to be higher or lower by some sort of scale, and those scales are subject to change. The nature of the scale at any given time can create conflicts between values. It is extremely important, therefore, that we look at the ordering or grouping of values in a culture or a person. Such groupings are called *value hierarchies*.

For instance, it is very difficult to be philanthropic at all times and assiduous in the collecting of art, stamps, or other possessions. Since both cost money, the one is likely to interfere with the pursuit of the other. To avoid conflict, ranking of interests is important. Thus, one man will be able to save his face, live in peace with his conscience, and live up to his ideals when he has been able to establish a value hierarchy in which philanthropy ranks, in crucial situations, somewhat higher than his interests in collections. The hierarchy of values is psychologically more important than the variety of values a person subscribes to. In one and the same culture most people will have the vast majority of leading values in common, but will be distinct from one another precisely in the rank given to each value in the individual value hierarchies.

Most of us in our culture rank the dignity and freedom of the individual very high, but certainly not all of us give it the top ranking it has among the rugged individualists. Pity for the deprived and concern for those who are handicapped in the economic struggle—in short, some sort of "brotherhood" idea—will be given a higher value-ranking yet by many people who maintain a high esteem for the dignity and freedom of the individual. To take a simpler case, the teen-ager who foregoes an evening meeting with his club in order to do a baby-sitting job with his younger siblings can be an excellent and ardent club member, but he ranks some family obligations still higher. And because of the different value placed on each pursuit, he can be at peace with himself and make a forthright choice without regret.

VALUE HIERARCHIES ARE DYNAMIC CONTROL DEVICES

In our discussion thus far, we have used the terms "peace," "conscience," "ideals," and "face saving." They refer to the inner relations which a person has with his value system. These relations are dynamic in the sense that they imply some degree of tension existing between his values and other pursuits of importance to him. The key idea to be grasped here is that man is a very complicated animal who is a product of both nature and nurture. Nature has endowed him with strong needs for food, shelter, pleasure seeking, sex, aggression, power, dominance over his environment, and urges to hurt and to kill which he can ignore only at the risk of failing to survive. Persistent interference with these instinctual needs stimulates anger, thirst for revenge, sadness, anxiety, or—in young children—temper tantrums. These are simple naturalistic events which can be easily observed. It is equally obvious and "natural," however, that an immediate and uncontrolled fulfillment of all these instinctual needs would lead to social chaos and a bloody battle for the survival of the fittest. And since man is a symbolic animal as well, his instinctual equipment drives him to seek such symbolic gratifications of sex, pleasure seeking, power, and aggression as are found in approval by his loved ones, acceptance by his peers, admiration from members of the opposite sex, social status and prestige, pride in his achievements, and confidence in his skills. All these are indispensable to a sense of well-being.

All natural, instinctual tendencies (and their extension into the symbolic realm) require control. Instinctual tendencies have power and a *general* direction or goal; they require control in the sense of regulation of the tempo and strength, and finer aiming (or deflection) in regard to the goal. And here is where a value system code book comes in handy—even though it be self-contradictory and conflictual. Without this, instinctual urges would lead to chaos not only for society but also for the individual, who would simply become the victim of his urges and fail to survive, because he would be unadapted to his world. For a part of man's natural equipment is itself contradictory. He has love and hate, and if, in a flare-up of hatred, he would hurt or kill his loved one who happens at one moment to deprive him, he would also hurt himself. Cain felt badly before he had slain his brother, but he felt *worse* after he had done so. Here is where nurture comes in as an aid to nature. Nurture in all its forms such as training, education, upbringing, parent-child relations, family structure, social patterns, culture, wisdom, humanism, religion, etc. provides for the controlling and harnessing and channelizing of nature so as to establish a workable and satisfying balance between the many opposing forces within the individual and between him and his world. This balance is to insure the survival of the individual as well as the group, and if possible to improve the lot and life chances of either. Moreover, because no one since Adam and Eve is born into a completely natural environment, everyone meets at birth an established social structure into which he will have to "fit," and the elements of nurture are themselves part of reality to which the individual must make his adaptations for survival.

VALUE HIERARCHIES ARE ACQUIRED BY LEARNING

Control, then, is a requirement of reality. There is always control somewhere and somehow, but not all control is effective, smooth, and productive. The degree and type of control grow and improve normally in the course of an individual's life. They also grow and become more refined in the life of a group or culture. At first, control tends to be mostly external. The hungry baby is controlled by his mother, who sets the feeding schedule. The shivering baby depends for his temperature control on the parents' pulling the blanket over him. His bladder and bowels are for some time uncontrolled and then controlled externally by the parents' demand for regularity. Anger is at first uncontrolled and shows up in persistent crying until the baby is red

or blue in the face, in temper tantrums, and in kicking and hurting; but these outbursts become quickly controlled by outside
forces which counteract the spontaneous outbursts. Then, in the
course of time, external controls give way to internal controls,
and most of that process is subsumed under the heading of
learning. Much of what is commonly called learning is a steady
internalizing of prescriptions and proscriptions originally coming from the outside. The young child depends on the "do's" and
"don'ts" of his parents and superiors; the older child and the
adult have replaced these by their own internal "do's" and
"don'ts." These are mediated by the conscience.

CONSCIENCE

The differences between "is" (nature) and "ought" (nurture)
are regulated, balanced, compromised, and made workable by
many subtle psychic processes and structures. Conscience has
been called of divine origin, directly implanted in the soul of
man, and it has also been described as the consensus of cultural
attitudes as interpreted by the individual.

Between these extremes lies the psychological conviction that
the individual's value system and hierarchy derive in very large
measure from the *early phases* of the process of internalizing
external controls. Our most important and powerful values (the
guiding principles for behavior) are the incorporated rules of
our parents. This works with great stringency precisely because
of our vast dependence upon them during the early years. We
want to become like them, we are perpetually urged to become
like them, and we copy their ideas and ideals so as to obtain
their approval, at first, and later our own self-approval. We also
copy their vices and prejudices. Our conscience comes to be a
kind of parent substitute, enabling us to give up the parents. To

be at peace with it means to us that we continue to be loved by the most important people in our life.

To be loved is to feel good. Hence, to be good is to be loved. To be loved, one must be lovable. And not to be good is to be unlovable and unloved. Not to be good, after the model of our most beloved caretakers and fellow men, creates a specific kind of anxiety which is known as guilt feeling. Behind guilt feelings lie apprehensive concerns that one is or will be punished, hurt, perhaps demolished.

The conscience is, then, a repository of early values. Since so much of it is due to a very early learning process, in which our discriminatory powers were not fully developed, there are many values firmly entrenched in conscience which cannot stand the test of reason. Unaware or insufficiently aware of their origins and nature, we hold fast to them at face value as "completely natural," "the normal thing to do," "obviously right (or wrong)," even when they are logically inconsistent or unjustifiable in the light of reason and present-day knowledge. There is a hard, irrational core in our conscience, which is rather difficult to undo or modify. Father Mailloux has called this "the archaic conscience."

But learning does not stop in the earliest phases of life. It continues for many years, hopefully throughout the course of life. Contacts with other beloved and significant people always make for some emulative changes in our values code. A stimulating teacher is emulated; religious, political, and scientific leaders declare positions or programs which make sense to us involving some alterations in our former "set" of concepts and feelings. But in making their ideas and ideals ours, thus letting them become a basis for our revised values, we tend to be increasingly choosy and discriminating; this is in part because as we have seen more of reality, we have learned to bargain with it in certain ways.

The newer values or value system modifications thus acquired tend to be more rational, more flexible and adaptive. A harsher word is "compromise." We continue to have pangs of anxiety when we fail to live up to our code, but this anxiety is subtly different from "guilt feelings." It is better described as a feeling of shame. It is not so much the transgressing of a hard and fast rule as the failure to live up to an ideal. We feel disappointed in ourselves, dejected. The threat of abandonment lurks in the background. We consider ourselves not quite fit for the exquisite company we keep.

Values, then, may be seen as forming a continuum. The irrational values of infancy, the strict, unquestioned internal "do's" and "don'ts" cluster at one end, and the more refined, flexible, more consciously held ideals at the other. The value hierarchy comprises the whole spectrum.

VARIETIES OF RELIGIOUS VALUE HIERARCHIES

And now we meet another serious difficulty. We have thus far looked at values in general. What about religious values in particular? What is their role in the value hierarchy? Are they all of one kind or are they diverse?

The difficulty is that religious instruction at home, in school, or in church tends to give by verbal definitions a strong priority to religious values. Religious people tend to feel that religion should determine the value hierarchy. Religion, to those people, is not one basis for value among many, but is *the* criterion to which all other criteria of value are subordinate. Some people go as far as saying that religion is the expression of a model value system from which all others are derived. Others would hold that religion consists precisely in the having of values, any at all, and that whatever values a man abides by, these constitute his religion. Our own definition of values as directive ideas for which one is willing to make a sacrifice, if need be, has some kinship with the latter viewpoint. When circumstances push sacrifice to the ultimate sacrifice of one's life, many people would automatically identify such a sacrifice as religious. None of these viewpoints is silly or unfounded, but one hits, of course, upon a serious philosophical and theological problem when the terms "religious" and "value" are found to overlap or interpenetrate so much.

Psychologically we should regard values, even when they refer to attitudes of deep concern to the individual who holds them, as criteria affecting the process of adaptation, and describe them neutrally. When we look at values scientifically, we find that for some people religious positions and practices are at the top of the value hierarchy, at least in what they say. Closer scrutiny may show that in their decisions and deeds they give greater importance to other values, or values from other sources or systems, for instance, capitalism, hedonism, or humanism. We will also find some people who deny being religious in any sense and who yet pursue an ideal of welfare for mankind with zeal and fervor involving what appears to be considerable sacrifice of ordinary personal satisfaction. We will find still others who show a rather inconsistent picture of religious zeal and charity at one time, or in one area of life, and cut-throat competition for the world's goods at other times or in other areas of life. We will find many people caught between the religiously oriented values to which they are committed and their desire for social approval. They must make daily compromises which do not quite fulfill either intention. The result is an uneasy, unstable, "hypocritical" life.

Since it is now a matter of public record, we may refer to the recent exposure of industrialists and business men who indulged in price-fixing. Whatever their private moral code, whatever their church affiliation and other evidence of value orientation might have been, the argument "business is business" was apparently able to nullify these values. Or consider the unethical machinations of certain labor union leaders who profess to be church-goers, lodge members, humanitarians, or supporters of great civic clubs. Indeed, it is particularly in the areas of one's daily work, one's choice of career, the way one earns a living, the management of gained or inherited capital, etc. that instability of values, value conflicts, and inadequate value hierarchies become exposed, if not publicly, then occasionally to oneself.

Even these sketchy observations suggest that the mere subscribing to religious values is in itself no guarantee for a good or worthy or integrated or healthy life. What is more, "religious values" is a very vague label which covers quite diverse content. There are as many religions as there are ideas about God and man. Some ideas about God, sincerely held by some as religious values, may be considered quite monstrous by others, equally religious, whose God concept and image of man is of a different breed.

Listening to what people say about their God, watching their faces in worship, hearing how they pray and what they pray for, and observing their daily life program can reveal curious versions of the meaning of religious values.

A God full of wrath and revenge, who has to be placated by continuous acts of humiliation and whose worship demands a stifling routine of elaborate rituals and laborious exercises, is likely to have worshippers who feel caught in the grip of a tyrant, who feel themselves at the mercy of an unpredictable, dangerous power. Where do such ideas of God come from? Very likely not from the major religious texts and catechisms, which are usually much more sophisticated, certainly not from the Bible; quite probably from the special religious culture and home environment to which the person belonged. They are the product of harsh, unloving but demanding parents, oppressive teachers, dull Sunday schools, stuffed-shirt ministers, and other advocates of a joyless life. Since *God is taught* he is always modelled in some measure after the human beings who portray him in word and deed to the child. And since parents are extremely important persons, a young child who depends on them is likely to attribute omnipotence, omniscience, and other features of greatness to them by virtue of which they come to resemble God. There is thus a double force at work connecting ideas of God and experiences with parents to one another.

By contrast, the idea of God may be kind, loving, and supportive, giving rise to good feelings and permeating the lives of his worshippers with a deep conviction of forgiveness, joy, purposiveness, self-regard, and a glad helpfulness towards others. The corresponding picture of man is encouraging: he is here for a purpose, to shoulder a task for which he has been given some degree of competence and some chance to succeed with God's help; he is worthy of love and has a measure of dignity because God's image is supposed to be alive in him. This religious value is likely to give rise to courageous attempts at improving the lot of mankind, producing a feeling of optimism. This religious value can be expected to stem from a home, school, or church in which the adults conveyed to the child a sense about his importance, lovableness, and worth.

For the sake of contrast, these two pictures are overdrawn. Some religious people will find serious fault with either, and rightly so, for in actual practice the situation is far more complicated. But the two extremes show plainly that religious values are very diverse and that one man's religion could well be called "unreligion" by a person of different convictions. Religion itself, as its history shows so clearly, ranges all the way from the primitive to the sophisticated, the horrible to the sublime, from constriction to freedom, from depressive to joyous, from belligerent to peaceful, from sick to healthy.

RELIGIOUS VALUES AND PERSONALITY INTEGRATION

Nearly all religions assert that their teachings involve the deepest meanings and the most unshakeable truths, man's highest divinely inspired values. But this is religion justifying itself and being measured by its own yardstick. Constructive religion will, of course, perpetuate its own constructiveness, and destructive religion its own destructiveness.

But there is one value point in the assertions of nearly all religions, the beauty of which is summed up by Paul Tillich. He defines faith as a state of "ultimate concern." This word *concern* (literally "bringing together") has many layers of meaning. One may take it as the bringing together of man and God, man and man, part and whole, surface and depth, rim and center, outside appearance and inner reality. Webster defines it, among others, as "affecting the welfare or happiness of . . ." and "care for any person or thing." Psychologically the term refers to a certain warmth of solicitude, an attitude of caring, a deep interest, sometimes anxiousness.

The preceding discussion suggests that a man's concerns or values are not only the controls of his behavior, but also devices for integrating his behavior, so that he will *perceive, think, feel, and act* as a whole, with all his "parts" participating. Those who say that religion tends to make a man "whole," meaning integrated and purposively co-ordinated, are not far off the mark.

But they speak idealistically, having in mind constructive religious teachings and values, which may indeed have this desired effect. Others may speak theologically, considering both the making and the "breaking" of man of divine importance. But, with a slippery change in emphasis, despair, mental torture, sickness, and *"dying of the flesh"* can become construed as religious ends in themselves, with little regard for eventual healing or wholeness. If this emphasis is pushed far enough, one may end up delighting in pain and having joy in suffering. Very often in our culture such ideas are pushed just far enough to produce a pervasive somberness or a chronic mild depression among many believers. This is different from finding some deep religious joy *despite* difficult and painful circumstances. In that case the "enjoyment of God" is preserved as the highest value in the value hierarchy, whereas pain and suffering have no value at all, or at best an indirect and instrumental "teaching value."

It seems very important then that religion be coupled with pleasure and enjoyment in order to fulfill its integrative role. Pleasure must be striven for as a high value, for its only alternative is unpleasure and adding the ideas of "depth" and "meaning" to it does not alter its sting. While the major faith groups in the Judaeo-Christian heritage come out frankly for combining God and pleasure, so that one well-known catechism defines the chief end of man as "to glorify God and enjoy him forever," the actual teachings within these faith groups sometimes portray a God so forbidding, revengeful, oppressive, and tyrannical that any enjoyment of him is impossible.

The same is true of man's concern for man. Man should enjoy his fellow man, not shy away from him or oppose him bitterly, nor, in our view, worship him. Next to God, man should be high in the value hierarchy of any person. While most religious documents assert this on religious grounds, psychologists have their own grounds for endorsing the prescription. It is a straight and plain observation that persons who love and like one another, who find their fulfillment in other people, will also find happiness for themselves. Conversely, most of those who are ill or seriously disturbed have deep-seated fears and suspicions of others, or harbor angry and revengeful feelings towards them. And most of the time they are deeply angry at themselves as well.

But it is also a common observation that in nominally religious homes and in schools, and even in churches, this prime value of mutual affection and enjoyment is not put into practice. It may be acclaimed; banal or sentimental words like "togetherness" and "fellowship" and "sociality" and "brotherhood" may be tossed about frequently. Inconsistently striven for or practiced, love is apt to be overshadowed by its opposite: hate-anger-fear. Think of the warped minds which look with horror or disdain on Negro fellow worshippers or those who justify their racial hatred policies by high-sounding biblical quotations! Or consider the glee with which so many of us talk about offenders being clapped in prison, there to be vengefully hurt, safely shielded from view and intentionally forgotten.

We believe it is also important that man have a healthy concern for himself. As we have noted before, one does find people who do seem to relate themselves to God in religious observances and who do seem to care for other people in many good thoughts and deeds, but have no regard for themselves and find little visible enjoyment in what they are doing "for God and their fellow men." They are making sacrifices all the time, out of a deep sense of duty, but without gladness. In the process they may be so duty-bound and preoccupied with sacrifice that they cannot fall asleep at night, lose appetite, and fail to keep themselves in working order. Their vitality wanes and they speak of themselves as worthless, no-good sinners. They seem to have a high place for God and others in their value hierarchy, but no place for "self" at all.

On closer examination one would find that God and other people were seen by such persons as frightening and very demanding, never content with their exertions. Even their loftiest thoughts and deeds were never good enough, in the eyes of God, parents, and other important persons in their lives. Thus having learned to think of themselves badly, they were also spurred on by a strict code of ethics to seek continually opportunities for making up, paying the price, or making atonement for their failures and shortcomings. One could also say that these "nice" people, who had learned so well their lesson of never being angry at others or God, of never swearing, of never even thinking badly of anyone, finally had no recourse but that of being deeply angry at themselves. Note that this is very different from the traditional Christian admonitions about having "sorrow for sin," "thinking lowly of oneself," or practicing "repentance," which are all balanced by the conviction that God is also merciful.

If religion is to foster man's sincerest enjoyment, if it is to stimulate his creativity and constructiveness, if it is to further the best in man and all nature, the value hierarchy of the religious man must comprise, next to God, one's fellow man and oneself at a rather high level. If it does not, a man's values may continue to be religious by somebody's definition, but they are not very constructive or helpful. They represent religion gone astray, "sick religion," or religion distorted by the shortsightedness, illness, warpedness, or misery of its user. For let us not forget that religion is *used*, that God is *taught and used*. They can thus also be misused or abused, and what seems at first sight a value in popular opinion may on closer inspection turn out to be a monstrous "un-value" or value distortion.

SPIRITUAL VALUES

After this discussion of religious values, some people would be inclined to make short shrift with spiritual values, saying that the latter will flow from the former, or be just a further specification of the religious ones. That course is too easy and fails to do justice to millions of people who would never admit to subscribing to any religion and yet embody great spiritual values, carried out in behavior. On the other hand, it is true that the term "spiritual" is a little shaky when its definition is not allowed to include formal religious elements. In ordinary language, however, the word is a shorthand expression for the many "higher cultural values" which can be found in ideas of general welfare, art, morality, "good causes," scientific exploration, medical care, and humanitarianism. There is a certain loftiness about such pursuits: they can be carried out with nobility, and often demand some sacrifice.

But with spiritual values too, we cannot simply acquiesce in just having, praising, or generally recommending them, but must look for a yardstick or touchstone for judging them in any particular individual. Lofty as art may be in itself, the pursuit of aesthetic values to the extreme can lead one into a world of unreality. Morality can be pushed to great extremes. The Romans had a clever phrase for this: *summum jus, summa injuria*. The highest justice may lead to the gravest injustice if the letter of the law, rather than its spirit, is followed. The shakiness of some "spiritual" values can be clearly seen in patriotism as practiced. While most of us would consider love of one's land, with the language and its customs, a high good and an important spiritual value which can lead to brave and noble deeds, this value is very often a deceptive control device for bad intentions or poor judgment. "Patriotism is the last refuge of a scoundrel," said Samuel

Johnson. Patriotism has all too often led to the oppression of those who happen to show love of their country in a different way. It was in the name of patriotism that the Nazis sent millions to the gas chambers; in its name the Spanish enslaved and murdered millions of Americans; in its name the Scots and English killed each other off for centuries; in its name a nation can make blunder after blunder in its relations to other countries, until the damage is irreparable.

Here again, we find use and misuse side by side. And again we must come back to the importance of the value hierarchy in the individual. When man's innate aggressiveness and his penchant for brute self-assertion are controlled by spiritual values of the kinds mentioned, everyone including the individual himself will benefit. As guideposts for behavior they take the sting out of man's uncultivated nature; they direct his energies to constructive goals and make it possible for him to relax his vigilance towards potential enemies. Spiritual values make it possible for a man to live on friendly terms with his culture and to foster its welfare because it is his welfare too.

But it would seem that each spiritual value, taken separately, or poorly placed in the value hierarchy, is no guarantee for anyone's welfare. Witness the examples of values-gone-wrong above. Spiritual values too must fit appropriately in the pyramid of all the values a man abides by, in such a way that the higher ones have, in crucial situations, preference over the lower ones. If morality is pursued frantically for its own sake and not controlled by an overarching love for mankind, one ends up in legalism, Phariseeism, or Philistinism. One will turn into a hypocrite. If it is pursued with magic or superstition, it can make one deeply depressed.

Here again, the touchstone of sincere pleasure and joy must be applied. Values have originated and are being remade every day for our benefit, not for our punishment. They are in the service of life, by controlling the dangers in human nature which may exterminate man. Being in the service of life, they have to grow and change with life. When they become frozen, they fail their purpose and turn into the same dangers they set out to check. They should enable man to realize his potentialities. They can do so only when they are organized into a value-hierarchy under the guiding value of love. This may mean, at times, the suspension of an important value for the sake of love.

In an attempt to formulate succinctly the main processes which foster health, Freud once said: to love and to work. We believe that Freud's dictum encompasses two of the highest values and behavior criteria. Theologians might add that they constitute the major categories of faith, the guiding principles of the Old and the New Testament.

Becoming the Complete Adult
Intimately

BECOMING
AN ADULT
SEXUALLY

by Ralph G. Eckert, Ph.D., former Head of
the Department of Child Development and
Family Relations, University of Connecticut,
Director of Counseling and Guidance Services,
Riverside County Schools, California

4

ONE becomes an adult *legally* by simply living twenty-one years. But when does one become an adult sexually? Sexual maturity involves the capacity to really love a person of the other sex and assume some responsibility for his or her life; an acceptance of one's own body and feelings, responsibility for one's own sexual behavior—and the consequences of it.

Just getting married does not make one sexually mature any more than having children makes one a loving and responsible parent. In the following pages we shall attempt to indicate some of the important steps by which we bring together and focus upon an individual of the other sex the great human need to love and feel loved, and the exciting sexual emotions. It is this combination of love and sex emotions, this ability to share these intense feelings with another human being, that makes some form of marriage and family life an accepted pattern of behavior in every social group studied by the social scientist.

Love and sex feelings are present in some degree in almost all interaction between the sexes, from the most fleeting interest in the other person to the most intense marital involvement. Because we can never really separate them, we shall use the

hyphenated term *love-sex feelings* to remind us that we are dealing with mixed emotions, and that it is often difficult to know
which is the dominant one. With most girls, the love emotions
seem to develop first, and stimulate the development of the sexual emotions. With boys, in general, the opposite seems the
normal course of development. One young woman probably
spoke for many whose teen-age marriages have failed when
she said, "I can see now that I married for romance and he married for sex. It just didn't work out."

Girls must learn that during their adolescent years boys'
sexual feelings are strong and easily aroused. Just looking at a
girl, or even thinking about having intercourse, may create an
exciting sensation in the genitals. If the girl by her behavior or
dress makes him think that intercourse with her might be a
possibility, the genitals may come into a state of expectant erec-
tion. It is very difficult for girls to understand this, for they
probably experience comparable feelings only after years of
maturing and experiencing an increasing response to physical
stimulation. Boys, on the other hand, find it almost impossible
to understand the girl's ability to enjoy the physical expressions
of affection without feeling any of the urges toward total intimacy which they experience so forcefully. Because in girls
sexual feelings are more generalized than genitalized, girls usually interpret what sex feelings they do have as love feelings and
think of marriage rather than sexual intimacy.

Love feelings, too, probably develop as a result of stimulation. As a child we need to receive love to feel good about
ourselves and to grow a healthy personality. As adults we need
to love if we are to continue to grow emotionally and spiritually.
Sexual emotions also seem to develop through fantasied as well
as actual physical contact between the sexes. None of us is fully
mature in either area at the time of marriage. But living to-

gether, provided that both emotions are somewhat developed, stimulates the further development of both love and sex feelings.

BUT NOT ALL HAVE POSITIVE LOVE-SEX FEELINGS

No, a child who is brought up without love feels very much as we feel when we are chilly. He craves the warmth of a loving person as we crave the glow of a cozy fire. If parents, teachers, and the "significant other" adults fail him, he increasingly turns a hostile face toward the world. The worse he feels, the worse he acts; the worse he acts the more he is rejected; the more he is rejected the worse he feels, and so on, unless someone breaks the vicious cycle. He comes not to expect love, and because of his hostile attitude he seldom gets it. He learns to *use* people rather than to care about them. *He* learns to pretend love to get sex; *she* learns to use sex to get at least a semblance of love. They may marry, but since each needs a kind of love the other cannot give, their marriage is almost doomed to failure—and their children almost doomed to grow up in the same loveless world their parents experienced. Fortunately, infants are so lovable that few adults fail to give them some of the love they so helplessly invite. So most of us have experienced some love, and we continue to seek it as long as we live.

Sex feelings are not likely to be linked with love feelings in adults for whom sex has been devalued by their parents or by their religion. If sexual pleasures are looked upon as lewd or indecent, the inevitable sex feelings we experience as human beings make us feel lewd, indecent, and unworthy. Any intimacy which creates or involves sex produces inner conflict. One girl who had learned about sexual intercourse from older youngsters in a disgusting way was shaken when she came to realize—as a pre-adolescent—that she herself was the result of intercourse.

After she had been treating her mother and father almost uncivilly for several days, her mother finally asked, "What in the world is wrong with you?" "Oh, Mother, how could you and Daddy do such an awful thing?" had been her agonizing inquiry.

Another girl, told only, "Never let a boy *touch* you or you may have a baby," developed a school phobia and refused to go to school when, in her first year of junior high, she had three young men teachers. When sex is feared, the coming of adolescence and the growth of sex feelings may create severe guilt and anxiety feelings. Such feelings can be relieved by patient counseling during which these fears can be *expressed* rather than *repressed*.

But love-sex feelings develop also in dating experiences with teen-agers of the other sex. Coeducation brings youngsters into stimulating contact with each other. Necking or "making out" is an adolescent version of the love-making they have observed on the screen a hundred times. Up to a certain point it may be a positive force in the development of desirable love-sex feelings which lead young adults into the responsibilities—and satisfactions—of marriage.

The danger of playing at love-making is that for adolescent boys, and adolescent men, the intense sexual feelings may propel them into total intimacy without much consideration of the possible consequences. And a girl who has never had enough appreciation and affection from her father may find male affection very satisfying. In her desire to reward the boy for the pleasure he is giving her, she may give him the physical pleasure he desires. She then finds herself torn between the powerful love-sex feelings which such intimacy normally generates in girls and equally intense fear and guilt feelings. If the former are stronger, the couple may be rushed into marriage before they are ready for it. If the guilt and fear feelings are stronger, the girl may break off the relationship, and find it more difficult later to trust her own love feelings—or those expressed by men.

We shall have happier marriages when there is less emphasis upon sex before marriage and more emphasis upon sex in marriage. Using the dating period to develop an enjoyable companionship with someone who enjoys the kind of people, thoughts, and activities that we do, and then adding to this already pleasant companionship the sexual intimacies of marriage should make possible a quality of marital happiness seldom possible to past generations. Intercourse is truly satisfying when it expresses the strong love-sex feelings of two people who enjoy each other so much they want to spend the rest of their life together.

WHAT ABOUT OUR "EARLY" MARRIAGES?

It is true that young people are marrying earlier than their parents' generation. Earlier dating has stimulated the earlier development of the love-sex feelings that lead to marriage. The automobile has freed young people from chaperonage and stimulated a more intimate type of dating. Movies and TV, repeatedly portraying all manner of love-making and all shades of intimacy short of total sexual intimacy, are a powerful influence. In girls, sexual feelings seem to be learned—largely as a result of physical stimulation. Because of the physical stimulation of modern dancing, the love-making that goes on in parked cars, and the more open expression of affection by adolescents for each other —even in the presence of adults—many girls develop earlier the intense love-sex feelings that lead them either into marriage or into premarital relationships.

Earlier marriages seem to be increasingly accepted by both

youngsters and adults. The successful invasion of the colleges by the postwar veteran and his wife destroyed the old belief that marriage and a college education didn't mix. Not only did the married veteran do better work than the unmarried veteran, but the veteran with children did best of all. The financial aid given the veteran—of both sexes—helped make college marriages economically possible and more prevalent.

As more jobs have been opened to women and there has been high employment except for periods of "recession," young women have taken jobs in ever increasing numbers. This has made it possible for them to help finance an earlier marriage than would otherwise be possible, whether their husband is also employed or is completing his education. With more men going on to college; with both high schools and colleges adjusted to the idea of married students; with more parents not only accepting early marriages, but actually subsidizing them—it is not surprising that the number of early marriages has steadily increased.

How Successful Are These Early Marriages?

That depends upon the couple's reason for marrying. Least successful, probably, are those marriages hastily arranged after a pregnancy has been determined. Christensen's study in Indiana would indicate that such marriages have about half as good a chance of avoiding divorce as the average marriage—that is, they have about a fifty-fifty chance of success. In an average courtship, the couple goes together about a year before becoming engaged, they are engaged an average of six months to a year before marriage, and they then have a year or two of marriage before the coming of children. In an unplanned pregnancy these two or three years of learning to get along and live together are telescoped into less than nine months. Instead of "growing together" in their thinking and feelings, they are "thrown together" with a host of problems and little time to adjust to them. It is not surprising that about half of such marriages end in divorce within five years. And even those that stay together may carry resentment through the years. She resents that she didn't have that beautiful church wedding she had always dreamed about—if they eloped to avoid delays or embarrassing haste. He may recall the first of every month, when the bills come in, that he had to drop out of school and take "just any job." Only by accepting equal responsibility for what happened (usually with the aid of a marriage counselor) can they face the future with optimism and a true acceptance of each other.

Almost equally difficult are the marriages where one or both have had continual conflict at home and have been anxious to "get away from it all." They often do not take time to really grow together before marriage. And their unhappy homes have not taught them, in a thousand day-to-day experiences, the art of living together harmoniously. All that is needed to insure failure is a romantic expectation that they "will live happily ever after." When they have problems, as all marriages do, they are likely to feel that their marriage was a mistake and want to try again with a different partner. Good counseling on their immediate problems and their long-range goals may help them find better solutions to their problems and better ways of working together so that they discover new levels of satisfaction in the marriage.

Another group of "high risk" marriages are those hastened by sexual tension. Their dates have involved more and more necking and petting, resulting in considerable sexual arousal. But they do not believe in premarital intercourse. To relieve the mounting sexual tensions they plan an early marriage. Not only do they shorten the time needed to really "grow to love" for each other, but the time they do spend together is sexually charged; they do not spend their hours together discussing the problems they will face in marriage and are unprepared for them. If their plans for an early marriage run into parental opposition they may elope. Not all elopements end in marriage failure, but a significantly higher percentage run into difficulty than those in which a fairly long dating and engagement period has led to a marriage approved by both sets of parents—and the community.

Still another high risk group are those who leave school to marry. During the war a big airplane manufacturing concern discovered that those who had not finished high school were not likely to complete their training program and remain long as valuable employees. This apparently applies to marriage too. The divorce rate seems to drop as the number of grades completed before leaving school increases. It is not assumed that formal education itself improves marriages, but that the person who disciplines himself and succeeds in school is also more likely to discipline himself and succeed at marriage. Those who "escape" from school by getting married are likely to find that marriage makes many more assignments than teachers do— particularly after the children arrive.

This is not to imply that everyone should go to college. Many would profit more and advance faster through on-the-job training. And many a girl who has satisfied the urge, or given in to the social pressure, to "go to college" by completing a year or two should have no compulsion to finish if both she and the man she is to marry are ready for marriage. However, such a decision should not be made impulsively. Counselors of adults find that many more regret not having stayed in school than regret having put off marriage as long as they did.

One other warning seems in order, for those who have dated

only the person they plan to marry. Two such couples come to mind. One couple discussed their situation with a counselor, who brought out into the open the problem that was in their mind: "How do you know that you are the best marriage partners for each other when you have never dated anyone else?" Instead of marrying at the end of their junior year in college, they agreed to break up and date others for six months. The boy had no difficulty getting other dates, but it was several months before other fellows began dating the girl. By the end of six months the boy was ready to go steady again, while the girl was enjoying "dating the field." But by November she accepted the boy's invitation for a date. At Christmas time they announced their engagement, and were married in June—just one year later and a lot more certain of each other than when they originally considered marriage.

The other couple married at nineteen after going steady for four years. The occasional quarrels which they thought marriage would eliminate increased instead. The girl became pregnant and could not finish the school year. Parents helped out financially, and the boy finished and got a job. But they always seemed to be in financial difficulty, and one set of parents or the other always came through in the pinch and saved them from the consequences of their own mismanagement. They eventually separated. Why?

Could it be that they were a couple of dependent personalities who started going together at fifteen—a couple of clinging vines who clung to each other? Could it be that four years of increasingly intimate necking and petting caused them to rush into marriage? Could it be that the unplanned pregnancy created a financial situation which wrecked the marriage, or was it their willingness to remain dependent on their parents and their parents' allowing them to remain so?

In conclusion, an early marriage is more likely to fail if it is an escape from an unhappy home, follows an unplanned pregnancy, is an escape from school, or is only a legally or socially acceptable way of consummating an increasingly intimate sexual relationship.

Early Marriages Can Succeed if Both Are Unusually Mature

How can we be sure we are unusually mature?

First, did we grow up in a family where the parents loved each other and their children? If children grow up seeing love freely expressed and experience love freely given, they come to see themselves as lovable human beings. Having grown up with parents who are sensitive to their needs—including their need for discipline—they learn to make the adjustments to authority and situations that life demands. Feeling good about themselves, they naturally feel good about others. Because their attempts to get love have been successful in their home, they reach out to others with the expectation of a positive response—and usually get it. They probably are ready for marriage earlier than most.

Secondly, we are mature to the degree that we have been taught—and have learned—to work for what we want. We give things and privileges to children freely. But the older we become the more the world expects us to be willing to work for what we want. Children who have been disciplined with love and encouraged to make a special effort to get a special reward have learned the satisfactions that come from self-disciplined effort, an experience often denied either the "spoiled brat" or the neglected child. We might ask ourselves: how realistically can we plan? How good are we at following through and completing planned projects? How easily are we diverted from long-range goals to more immediate pleasures?

Thirdly, have we learned to earn and manage money? One girl who was being graduated in nursing was anxious to get some professional experience and some extra cash before starting her family. "You understand," she said to her fiancé, "that I plan to work several years before starting a family don't you?" "Oh sure, baby," he had replied, "I'm counting on that." As it turned out, he quit his part-time job so that he could devote all his time to his studies in graduate school. Have we moved, in one generation, from a masculine pattern, which made it difficult for men to allow their wives to work, to men who expect it? (Incidentally, that marriage failed.) Modern marriage permits both men and women to help finance the marriage, and it expects them both to help in the home.

Fourthly, are we prepared to carry our share of the work that goes into successful homemaking? No doubt the marriage above failed in part because the man expected his wife to carry two jobs (breadwinner and homemaker) while he carried only one (student). That marriage might have succeeded (as many marriages where the wife is the breadwinner do) if the man had been willing and able to carry his share of the homemaking. The studies of happy marriages show the men helping more with the children, more with the dishes, more with the buying and cleaning—whether the wife works outside the home or not. Not only does it equalize the load, but working together on tasks promotes companionship and leaves the wife freer to join in recreation (and not too fatigued or irritated to be a good sex partner). He would probably also suffer from guilt feelings if she carried two jobs and he only one, and would project this guilt by reacting "unreasonably" when she turned on the vacuum cleaner while he was watching television, etc.

And finally, these early marriages are more likely to succeed if the couple have time to get adjusted to each other and to get on their feet financially before their lives are complicated by pregnancy and the arrival of a child. A realistic program of birth control makes it possible, for example, for both to work part time and both to continue their schooling. They may have to lighten their program a bit and even take an extra year to finish. But if they are enjoying a really satisfying companionship and learning to share the planning and the homemaking, their marriage may be off to a good start.

WHAT ARE SOME OF THE ALTERNATIVES
TO EARLY MARRIAGES?

That depends, of course, upon the causes of the early marriages. We can reduce the number of young people who rush into marriage to escape from unhappy homes by helping this generation of parents to have happier homes. We can reduce the number of young people who escape from school into marriage by injecting into the curriculum of the junior and senior high schools more study of the personal adjustment problems all youngsters have in learning to get along with their parents, their friends, and the other sex, and in preparing for marriage and the problems that it will bring. We can help teachers realize that good teaching in the junior and senior high schools requires a vital understanding of adolescents and their problems as well as their subject area skills. But these things will not happen in time to help today's young people with their problems, so let's discuss some immediate alternatives to early marriage.

Don't Let Sex Rush You into Marriage

The old idea that the male possesses a powerful *sex drive* that must have some outlet has been pretty much exploded by Kinsey's study of prison populations and Wetherill's study of adolescent boys. The so-called sex drive seems to be largely the result of thinking about and desiring sexual orgasm rather than vice versa as has been supposed. Let's face it: the sexual orgasm, particularly when it is preceded by exciting and pleasurable sex play, is the most thrilling and engulfing physical sensation most human beings ever experience. What more explanation do we need to account for the widespread interest in sex? Were sexual pleasure not related to human reproduction, it would certainly have no rival as our favorite pastime. But since it is, and since women bear the children, women have always felt differently about sex from the way men have felt. Mothers start early to impress their daughters with this fact to keep them from becoming mothers at fourteen—as is normal in some cultures. Add to this inhibiting fear of pregnancy the fact that the female initially experiences sexual excitement more generally, becomes aroused more slowly, is more cyclical in her sexual feelings because of her menstrual cycle, and that she finds it more difficult to separate sex and love, and we have quite sufficient explanation for the fact that women feel differently about sex from the way men feel.

There is also great individual variation within each sex. Individual excitability seems closely related to the general energy level and the tension under which the individual lives. Sex play brings about a build-up of tension which the orgasm convulsively releases. Electrical impulses fan out over our entire body with pleasurable sensations focalizing in the genital area. In addition, women in particular relate sexual activities to other psychological needs. A woman may use sex to express love; to reward or punish either her sex partner or herself; to express rebellion against or conformity to existing moral attitudes; and so on. Because her sexual feelings are experienced as more

generalized excitement, she can interpret them in more generalized ways.

In addition, both sexes use sex to fulfil other personality
needs. The girl who is unsure of her ability to elicit love because
she has never been able to win the love of her father often uses
sex to get the love she is not sure she can get otherwise. The
boy who needs to hurt women because his own mother rejected
him may become a first class wolf, thus satisfying both his desire for a sex thrill and his need to hurt women. Kinsey reports
men who pretend avid love—sometimes really feel it—for a
woman until she "gives in" and then lose all interest in her and
seek out other victims. We probably all use sex to some extent
to satisfy other than purely sexual desires and needs. But the
conscious direction of love-sex feelings toward marriage, children, and stable and enjoyable family life seems to be our most
rewarding achievement.

Let's Talk about Masturbation

On my shelf is a book entitled *Satan in Society*. Written about
eighty years ago and before the germ theory of disease had been
established, it blames many illnesses upon the "self-abuse" this
physician found many of his patients were practicing. Witnessing masturbation in institutions for the insane and the feeble-
minded, he blamed these mental conditions too upon "self-
abuse." Some still believe masturbation is physically or mentally
harmful, in spite of the mountain of evidence to the contrary.
Practically all normal males have masturbated frequently—
some daily—with no harmful results. Any harmful effects are
entirely psychological, such as the guilt feelings some experience,
the promiscuity sexual fantasy might encourage, and so forth.

But it is probably time to recognize that masturbation may
serve some worthwhile functions in our society: as a form of

sexual release for tensions created by our erotically-romantically oriented entertainment; or as motivation toward marriage when intercourse is fantasied with an admired member of the other sex. It is possible to become preoccupied with self-stimulation; fantasy may become a substitute for real companionship with the other sex, but apparently seldom does for a well-adjusted person. It is probably also a pleasant and harmless way to relieve the sexual tensions aroused by erotic literature, pictures, sexually oriented conversation or jokes, and the physical contacts of dancing, necking, etc. Releasing tensions stimulated by contact with the other sex on a date may allow the young man or woman to relax into sleep more quickly and soundly, and may reduce the drive toward an early and sexually oriented marriage or the drift toward premarital relations.

What about Petting to Orgasm?

Some couples feel that petting to orgasm permits them to experience many of the satisfactions of intercourse without running the risk of pregnancy or of losing respect for each other. Others feel that this is "going too far," that such intense involvement and familiarity with each other breaks down resistance to intercourse, which often follows. While self-respect and respect for the other is less likely to be damaged than by intercourse, petting to orgasm is probably more satisfying to the girl than to the boy. She is more likely to be satisfied to continue the relationship while he is even more motivated to achieve complete sexual union, and this puts a strain on their relations. She may come to feel that he is being unreasonably persistent about going all the way; he may become resentful and exploitive because he feels she is getting satisfaction and he isn't. What might have been a successful courtship and marriage ends in resentment and disillusionment for some.

Counselors differ in regard to petting to orgasm. A few encourage it for a couple about to be married. They feel it may be
a gradual step toward union, so that the girl may approach her
wedding night with more pleasant anticipation and less anxiety.
Most feel that intense sexual involvement should be reserved
for marriage; that this period before marriage is needed for planning and dreaming about the future and considering the many
problems that marriage will bring that might otherwise be
neglected. They insist that sexual orgasm intensifies rather than
reduces sexual desire, and encourages either earlier marriage or
premarital intercourse. "Letting go" to the point of orgasm while
drawing the line against complete involvement is a fine line that
probably few couples can follow long.

How Can We Be Affectionate
and Still Avoid Sexual Stimulation?

We can't, entirely. The physical contact and generalized thrill
of an affectionate kiss or hug is very pleasant and therefore
makes for good feeling between the two. Continued for very
long, this generalized sexual response becomes *genitalized*. This
happens first to the male, and this is the place to call a halt
unless he really wants to get his partner sexually involved. If he
persists, he usually becomes tense and restless—particularly his
hands get restless. This should warn the thoughtful girl that he
is no longer thinking of her in terms of friendship, love, and
marriage, and if she wants to get him back on that track it is
wise to call a halt to the love-making and suggest something
else. As one girl put it, "Any girl can pet, but a smart girl can
always think of something better to do." If the girl continues
being affectionate until her own generalized sexual feelings
become genitalized she is in double trouble. Not only is the man
highly motivated toward intercourse—a man she would like to

please—but she herself now has the same feelings. She may find that, like the trans-Atlantic flier, she has passed the point of no return.

A couple genuinely anxious to build a successful marriage need to explore many areas of life if they are to enter marriage confident that they really want the same things, that they like the same types of people and activities, and that they can discuss and solve problems through discussion. It seems wise to be so busy having a good time together, so busy planning and discussing their future together, during the final stages of courtship that they do not allow themselves to become involved in the prolonged affection-giving that produces intense sexual arousal. If they really care enough about each other and their future, they will not find it too difficult to express lots of genuine affection for each other without experiencing too much sexual stimulation. Avoiding prolonged kisses or periods of affection-giving is often all that is necessary.

What Kind of Goals Make It Easier to Wait?

To really love someone is to put his or her happiness and welfare ahead of our own. Too often, when counseling with a couple rushing into marriage (or a couple whose marriage is shaky), I have felt that each was saying, not "I love this person," but "I want this person." There is a real difference. She was not saying, "I want what is best for him," when she was willing for him to drop out of school so that they could be married. And he was not saying, "I want what is best for her," when he was willing to have her drop out of school and help support him while he got an education.

Goals that go beyond the wedding and the honeymoon help. Some couples are so busy planning for the wedding and honeymoon that they don't have time to plan for the marriage. A long-range plan makes it easier to say, "What's the hurry?" With fifty years of marriage ahead, it is easier to take another six months or a year to really prepare for marriage. Marriage involves jobs, homes, children, and all of the things that go into family living. Not being willing to settle for just any job, but waiting to get the education you need or a job with a real future, may pay off well in the long run. Too many couples rush into marriage as soon as they both get jobs and can finance a prolonged honeymoon. When she finds herself pregnant and has to stop work—when they have to cut to one income at the very time doctor and hospital bills come in, and it is desirable or even necessary for them to move to a larger apartment or house —many couples wish that they had waited. Few couples ever regret that they waited to finish school or to see something of the world before getting "tied down" with family responsibilities. One doesn't feel tied down when one is really ready to settle down.

How Long Is It Wise to Go Steady? To Be Engaged?

It is not so much a matter of *how long* you go with someone as *how well* you get to know him. Divorce is less likely to occur if the couple have known each other for at least a year or two before marriage. If they dated a long time before becoming engaged, then the engagement itself need not be so long. But again, it isn't just going together and having fun together that make a good courtship; it is having a wide variety of experiences, meeting and working out together a variety of problems, and learning to respect each other. It is also important to get to know each other's families. You don't just marry a person, you marry "the whole darn family." It is important to observe how your future mate relates to each member of his family. Watch how his mother "mothers" him, for he may expect the same from you. Observe his father and how he fills his role, for your future husband has learned to be both a husband and a father from him. In the same way, your fiancé will have learned to be a wife and mother from her mother, and how to relate to men and what to expect of them from her father. If she gets on well with her brothers and sisters, she will probably get along well with people generally; if she doesn't, she may have trouble doing so.

Too much affection-giving leading to the mounting of physical tensions is a major problem in both steady dating and engagement. Too much intimacy rushes people into marriage. Not seeing each other *too often* and not being *too affectionate* make it possible for some engagements to go on for years without too much strain. Discovering new psychological interests rather than stimulating physical attraction makes for longer engagements and more successful marriages.

HOW LONG DOES IT TAKE TO REALLY "GROW TO LOVE"?

Lincoln once commented that a man's height was not so important as it was that his legs were long enough to reach the ground. The same applies to marriage. Before moving from steady dating to engagement, and from engagement to marriage, a couple should take time to:

Really Get to Know Each Other as Persons

"Falling in love" is often being in love with love rather than with a person, being in love with a dream we have created in our own mind. Getting to really know a person takes time—and talk. You need to know what he (or she) thinks and how he feels about a lot of things, and to do this you must see how he acts in a lot of situations. That is the real test of what a person is—what he wants, what he needs to be happy.

Discover or Develop Common Goals

What do you both believe in, want, or need to be happy? It is easy to verbalize dreams, but the real test of your values is: What will you two work for, save for, and pray for during your engagement and the years ahead? Do you value the same things, or are you learning to do so as you dream and plan together?

Learn to Care about, and Not Just "Want," This Human Being

We like people *because,* but we love people *in spite of,* their human weaknesses. Growing to love a person involves getting to know that he is not perfect, to foresee the kind of problems that the inevitable difference of personalities and backgrounds will cause in the day-to-day problems of living together, and still care enough about the other person to want to spend the rest of your life together.

Really Care about the Other Sexually

Everyone wants sexual pleasure in marriage. But a mature person's pleasure is heightened by also being able to give pleasure. Only then will sex be a *strength* rather than a *problem* in the marriage. Only then will sex be both a physical thrill and an expression of love. Only as you really love will sex not be used selfishly or as a reward for good behavior (and withheld when you want to punish your mate—a real source of irritation in many marriages). Do you care enough about the other's happiness to read some good books and try to understand the other sex so that you may more surely satisfy your partner's basic needs?

Neither Devalue nor Overvalue Sex

Most important, perhaps, do you both value sex about equally? How do you know? How can you know until you have lived together for years? There are no easy answers. But you can discuss sex honestly; and even better, you can discuss your feelings honestly with a marriage counselor before you marry. His work with marriages in difficulty makes him keenly aware of the attitudes that make trouble and the knowledge that helps couples achieve a more satisfying relationship. Feelings of which we are unconscious often get in the way. Becoming conscious of them gives us more control over them.

Sex is very important in the early years of marriage, but with the passing of years it has to share honors with children, homes, jobs, and community responsibilities. Sex can attract people into marriage, but it isn't enough to hold them together. Sex is important, but so are other things. The mature person who really cares about his mate can balance these. A good courtship is one in which two people discover that they like many of the same things and the same people and believe pretty much the same things, or one in which they discover in time that they don't.

HOW CAN ONE "BECOME" THE RIGHT PERSON AND THEN FIND THE "BEST" PERSON?

Being the right person is more important than *finding* the right person. We tend to be attracted to someone who seems to satisfy our most pressing emotional needs. We tend to marry someone who is strong where we feel inadequate, and who is weakest where we feel strong. This makes us important to each other. The person who doesn't have too much self-confidence is

attracted to someone who does. The person who finds it difficult
to make up his mind is attracted to someone who can, and so
on. People who admire our strengths make us feel good about
ourselves and about them.

But love involves much more than just responding to the
good feelings someone has for us (infatuation). Loving is caring
about people—all people—because someone first cared about
us. *Growing to love* involves going together, being engaged, living together in marriage, having children together, and caring
about the other's desires and needs as you work together to
solve the many problems of family living. Most people probably marry on a combination of ego satisfaction, sex attraction,
and the beginnings of love. And this is probably enough to get
married on *if* both are the kind of people who can grow to care
deeply about another human being. Some have learned to be
loving and appreciative because someone loved and appreciated
them. But we can all learn to be that way, or more that way,
by consciously trying to be appreciative, kind, thoughtful, and
helpful and experiencing both the inner satisfaction it gives us
and the kind of response it brings from others.

You can also become the right person by taking the initiative
in having wholesome dating experiences with a variety of personalities before you allow yourself to become too serious with
one. You can be yourself, which lets others be themselves. You
can avoid trying to impress people, realizing that we make the
best impression when we *are impressed* by and interested in
another human being. You can show consideration for both
families by spending time with both families and trying to enjoy
your fiancé's family. It will be your family too, after you marry.

How Intimate Dare One Become during the Engagement?

How intimate do you want to become? Most women have grown up associating intercourse with marriage. Marriage means living together, with intercourse now not only permitted but taken for granted. Has marriage lost some of its significance if intercourse begins before marriage? Apparently most women think so and prefer to wait.

Most men also really prefer not to have intercourse with a woman they really love before marriage. Even men who have been rather exploitive in their attitude toward women generally feel different about the girl they are to marry, and one might almost say the more a man loves a woman the less he desires to have intercourse with her before marriage. Yet many men and women who do not really believe in intercourse before marriage drift into it—and then regret it. How does this happen, and why?

When a woman loves a man she wants to be close to him, to be loved and caressed by him. She enjoys the euphoric feelings that engulf her and feels that she is very much in love. She does not realize that these feelings are partly her generalized sexual response to the male. The man too has these feelings, for the intimate contacts with a woman's body are highly stimulating to him. The more aroused they both become the more likely they are to allow their sex feelings to override their love feelings and to begin to rationalize total intimacy. After all, we're engaged, we love each other—why wait? A counselor might, if he were consulted, remind them that only a little over half of all engagements end in marriage, and that too much emphasis upon sex during the engagement apparently causes many broken engagements. The conflict *within* each, the desire for total intimacy and the desire not to have total intimacy before marriage, often flares up as conflict *between* them. "What's wrong with us," one couple asked. "We fight over the least little thing. Then the next day, after we calm down, it seems silly. One or the other calls up and apologizes and we are both sorry. But the next date it is some other silly quarrel. Do we really love each other or what's wrong?"

Nothing was wrong except that they were so intimately affectionate with each other that sexual tensions became generalized tensions which made them irritable and jumpy. In other cases, girls who have limited boys strictly to affection-giving, once engaged, feel that they may permit their fiancé almost any freedom short of intercourse. Some girls who are able to hold the line sexually cannot, however, control their emotions; and eventually they relieve their tensions with crying spells, either with their fiance or after their date is over. Even engaged couples who genuinely love each other find it necessary to limit the amount and kind of affection they express for each other if they do not want total intimacy before marriage. For uncontrolled love-sex feelings lead naturally to total intimacy.

One girl reported having agreed to intercourse, when she was suddenly shocked by what she was about to do. She turned furiously upon her fiance and told him she hated him and that he obviously didn't love her or he wouldn't suggest such a thing. It took him six months, and the help of a counselor, to win her back and convince her that they really loved each other. Another girl, who did not experience the shock and revulsion until the next morning, also broke off the engagement. Others have the same reaction but feel so involved—so "trapped," as one expressed it—that they have to go through with the marriage, and the sooner the better. She suggests setting a date. "What's the hurry?" may well be his reaction. If they continue to have intercourse, apparently her drive toward marriage is increased. At the same time, his seems to decrease. One of his motives for marriage is a release of sexual tension. If he is relieving it rather regularly, he may not be so anxious to marry and take on all the responsibilities and problems of marriage. She begins to wonder whether he loves her or sex!

Apparently, too, another unconscious force is set in motion. Boys learn about sex mostly from other boys who talk about sex to get attention or to enjoy the sexual stimulation they get from just talking about sex. The boy grows up unconsciously dividing women into two groups: the nice women, like his mother and sisters, who do not have intercourse outside of marriage; and "sexy women," whom men play around with until they are ready to marry a virgin. Apparently, a man who begins having intercourse with a woman he thinks he loves unconsciously moves her from the group of women who are not available as sex partners (the kind men marry) to the group who are. Perhaps he loses some of his respect for her. Perhaps he has unconscious guilt feelings which he projects outwardly at her; if she hadn't given in, he wouldn't have had these feelings. Whatever the cause, he often begins to see faults in her he hadn't observed before. He begins to resent the little demands she makes upon him, the things she takes for granted. He begins to wonder whether he really loves her, whether he should go through with the marriage. "She says if I don't marry her now I'm a heel," one young man told his counselor. "I don't want to be a heel, but neither do I want to marry someone I don't love any more."

With good counseling, such young men can be helped to analyze their own feelings, and trace the changes that transformed them from ardent lovers to reluctant and confused ex-lovers. And they can be helped to understand that women's reactions are literally the opposite of men's, that is, the more they love the more they desire total intimacy; that she gave in only because she loved him so much, and he seemed to desire it so much; and that, for her, intercourse is not something lewd or lustful, but a beautiful expression of her complete love for and trust in him. Given this help in understanding his own and his fiancé's reactions, his feelings often change, and he is eager to go ahead with plans for the marriage.

But if he does not get this help, his doubts may grow. One such young man discussed his doubts with a counselor, but omitted any facts relating to sexual intimacy. Finally the counselor asked how long they had been having intercourse.

"What makes you think we have?" the young man asked in surprise.

"Well you've been going together nearly two years, you've been engaged for nearly a year, and now recently you have begun to doubt your love for her. The most logical explanation is that you have begun having sex relations." He reluctantly admitted several months of intimate relations.

"Had she ever had intercourse with anyone before?"

"She said she hadn't."

"Did you believe her?"

"I did then, but now I don't know."

When the counselor talked to the girl next day, she too had begun to doubt. Did he really love *her*—or sex? After the counselor discussed with them the chain reactions described above, their attitudes began to change. After several conferences their confidence in each other had grown to the place where they began again to plan on marriage. But will they ever have as much faith in each other as they might have if they had waited until they were married to be completely intimate with each other? Who knows? The Kinsey studies show that men and women who have had premarital sex relations are twice as likely to have extramarital as those who have not. And faith is very important to marriage, particularly to men. For as one man put it, "A woman knows it's her child, but a man can only have faith it is his." Male-dominated societies have always forced a moral code upon women which the men themselves do not always follow!

Can the Engagement "Predict" the Marriage?

A group of students were asking how it is possible to know whether it is love or just infatuation or physical attraction. "How did you know, Norma?" one of them asked a married student.

"Well at first I wasn't sure. When he asked me to marry him I was thrilled but also scared. I told him that I liked him better than any boy I'd ever gone with and that he was a wonderful escort at parties, but that since I had never seen him in a family situation I couldn't be sure what kind of a husband or father he would be. So we agreed that, instead of going out on dates, he should come over after work several times a week and have dinner with the family and then we would spend the evening at home. I was pleased when he got right in and helped with a few things. He got along with my parents, and we had fun with the kids. Sometimes we would just listen to music, watch TV, or read. After several months of having many of our dates at home, I had a pretty good idea what kind of husband he would be."

Much can be learned by seeing how a boy relates to his mother and his sisters or how a girl "handles" her father and brothers; how they treat younger brothers and sisters and how the kids feel about them; what the family does for recreation; and whether emotions are freely expressed or bottled up.

Engagement gives us the right to spend whole week ends with each other's families—learning to make some of the many adjustments we all have to make if we are to survive as members of the family clan. Learning to enjoy the family fun that our fiancé enjoys helps prepare us to have more fun in our own family.

HOW READY ARE YOU TO HANDLE
THE SITUATIONS OF MARRIAGE TOGETHER?

1. Are you expecting too much of sex in marriage? Some imagine that the wedding ceremony automatically opens the door to sexual bliss. Not so. No two men or women are the same, and each couple will need time and mutual consideration to explore the many possibilities open to them. Read more than one good book on sex, and then let the woman take some initiative. She knows what pleases and excites her most. Most men find intercourse about the nicest thing that ever happens to them. For women, the sex response is a learned one. But most of them can learn to enjoy sex as much as men, if they really want to.

2. Can you really disagree and accept your differences? If there are no differences, only one person is thinking. If differences are too painful, neither thinks; they just feel. These unexpressed feelings become blocks to understanding. Remember, it takes a lot of talking to make democracy work in the family or anywhere else. When we are tempted to insist on getting our way, let's hope that a still small voice rises up in us to ask, "Do you want that kind of a marriage?" Being willing to give in on less important things makes it easier for you to be a bit insistent about the things that are really important to you. It's good to disagree about things that you don't have to act on, such as what the President should be doing about the world situation. It is good for children to learn that people can disagree and still love each other. It helps them to realize that there is no one answer to most problems, to be more open-minded, and to be more spontaneously alive.

3. And closely related, dare you express angry feelings once in a while, confident that you can make up? Most irritations are due to misunderstanding or looking at situations exclusively from our own point of view. One of the values of counseling is that you can express angry feelings without having someone else getting angry and firing back. Being genuinely sorry about the misunderstanding, or sorry that you did something that was irritating, helps ease the tension. Taking full responsibility for what happened is the best way to make it easy for the other to admit his contribution to the misunderstanding. If we *listen* rather than attempt to justify or defend what we did, we often get new insight that helps us avoid future misunderstandings.

4. Can you plan together and then follow through? Learn to pin down who is going to do what. Often we plan, and each assumes the other is going to do something. Neither does. Each tends to blame the other when nothing happens. Pin it down. Then most of us need a reminder . . . "When are you planning to. . . . ?" Say, "Thanks for reminding me." We might have forgotten and then felt terrible. We might have projected our guilt as hostility—"You should have reminded me." It's tough if our mate gets irritated when we remind him, and also if we don't.

5. Have you learned to make good use of money? There will never be enough for all the things we want to have or do. Before you get married, get a good book on personal and family spending. Read it and keep it around to help settle arguments later. Determine to help each other get ego satisfaction through praise and appreciation—and, of course, real success. Trying to get ego satisfaction by impressing people with what we have or what we spend usually fails, and we are in trouble financially to boot.

6. How successful have you been in growing to love your in-laws? The average person reflects the way he is treated. If someone is nice to him, he is nice too. If someone is nasty, so is he.

The mature person takes the initiative in being kind and thought-ful. Most people like the person who treats them that way and respond in kind.

7. And finally, have you realistic plans for your marriage? It takes a lot of honest discussion to turn dreams into plans. How are you going to finance the marriage if she becomes pregnant and has to give up her pay check just when expenses mount? Who is going to be primarily responsible for such household chores as paying the bills, balancing the checkbook, and making out the income tax? Usually the woman takes the responsibility, and the man helps with such specific things as balancing the checkbook or making out the income tax. Most couples now use a joint checking account and share the responsibility of keeping about one month's salary in the account. It gives you security and saves money to keep a sizable balance.

Have you made fairly realistic plans about buying or renting a home, riding the buses or buying a used car? You can save a lot by learning to resist the organized attempts to stimulate "impulsive buying." Planning together and making any major purchase only after discussing it with one another helps to pre-vent impulse buying and to prevent conflict and financial prob-lems as well.

ARE YOU READY TO MAKE
THE MOST OF YOUR MARRIAGE?

Will your dreams come true? Not entirely. They never do. Each person faces the future with a set of dreams. In marriage there are two sets of dreams, and neither will come true. But just as "truth is stranger than fiction," what will happen may be even better than either dreamed *if* neither tries to impose his dream on the other; *if* they face the future as an unwritten book which they will write together from day to day, month to month, year to year, as they live it. Each day, each month, and each year will bring unexpected problems. But happiness is not an absence of problems. Happiness comes as we tackle each day and its problems in a spirit of adventure and confidence. Creativity is finding new solutions to both old and new problems— better solutions than we would have found last month or last year, because we have more experience and more maturity with which to tackle them.

We find new and exciting solutions in proportion as we free each other to approach each problem creatively. If we fear that an idea will be greeted with, "How ridiculous can you get?" many truly creative ideas will never see the light of day. But if we respect each other and the great reservoir of experience stored in our unconscious minds, then each will feel free to toss out any idea that comes to mind. It may be completely impractical but still have a spark of creativity that sets off a host of related ideas which, after a lively or even heated discussion, become a plan of action—*our* plan of action. Only then can we free ourselves from the bondage of past dreams and make the most of *our* marriage. Only then will we have become truly adult, sexually, ready to play our role as husband or wife, father or mother.

Becoming the Complete Adult
Intellectually

THE
MEANING
OF EDUCATION

by Harold Taylor, Ph.D., author, educator,
former President of Sarah Lawrence College
in Bronxville, New York

5

I CAN remember the excitement of my first day at school, and I recall it every time I smell that odd mixture of new varnish, floor seal, disinfectant, and indoor air which makes up the smell of school at the opening of term. The excitement was composed partly of fear of the unknown, anticipation of an experience which was about to happen and was long overdue, anxiety over whether I would be able to do what was asked of me, and a feeling of a peculiar kind of loneliness which had to do with an idea that somehow I was leaving home forever. I recall having had the same sense of excitement on going to high school, for most of the same reasons, except that instead of the twinge of loneliness for home there was loneliness for the school I was leaving.

The first day of college was a different kind of experience, with the same excitement that something was about to happen, but with no regret about leaving the past. The past was complete in itself, with its own triumphs and disasters, victories and defeats. They all belonged together—the examinations, the football team, the classes, the teachers, the subjects, the orchestra, the parties, the talks about dental health—and they all finished together. I entered the next phase of my life with very little knowledge of what it might contain. I knew only that college would be different from high school and that I was to go because my teachers had said so to my parents, and we had somehow found the money for the first term's tuition. I had no problem about choosing a college, because there was only one choice— the one to which I could ride or walk from home.

I therefore went on opening day, handed in my registration card, paid my tuition, and stood in line to meet the Registrar. When my turn came he looked up from the card he was holding and asked, "What do you want to be?" "A writer," I replied, having decided that question at the age of ten, after reading Robert Louis Stevenson. "You should take the course in Philosophy with an English or History option." "Yes, sir," I said, and thus became a philosophy student.

I did not dare ask what philosophy was, or why I should study it, although I knew it was something philosophers did and that it had to do with the mind; at that age I had never been able to discover why the study of the particular problems philosophers chose to deal with was of importance to anyone but philosophers. I remained in that condition for the four years of college, did what I was asked to do, and was graduated as a philosophy student. It was not until two years later, in England, where I continued to study philosophy (still under the Registrar's influence, I gather, and still assuming I was to be a writer) that I discovered the relevance of philosophy to my own life, and discovered at the same time what my education had been intended to do.

Looking back on it now, to that first day when I entered the anonymous society of adults, that is to say, the company of whatever kind of adult one becomes by ceasing to be a high school student, I find that I had simply been placed in a network of academic studies whose purpose everyone assumed but nobody mentioned. We were there to get a college education, and a college education consisted in taking the courses set out in the curriculum, meeting many other people of the same age, being an athlete, and enjoying the life of the campus.

In some ways, the absence of any direct awareness of the meaning of my education was a blessing, since it saved me from the throes of anxiety about whether I was doing the right things by which to achieve my intellecual manhood. I assumed that I was, had no cause to question it, and lived a fairly uncomplicated and full life while a new self quietly grew in place of the one I had left behind in high school. I read widely, both inside and outside the curriculum, more outside than in, became seriously interested in contemporary literature, and let the future take care of itself.

INSTITUTIONS OF EDUCATION

This, and my experience in education since then, have given me strong views about the relation of education to life. In the first place, it has led me to believe that the closer education stays to life, the better it is likely to be. By this I mean that life as it is lived from day to day is the ultimate source of what people learn and what they learn to believe. Children learn to behave in one way or another because of the examples and standards of behavior they see around them from morning until night. They are natural learners who learn all the time. They enjoy learning, whether it is learning to ride a bicycle, play a game, or read a book. It seems to me just as foolish to teach a child to think by telling him what other people have thought as it is to teach a child to ski by having him read a book about it. For skiing, what is needed is the practice of wearing skis while going up and down hills with a good skier who can coach the learner. For thinking, what is needed is a field of ideas and a good scholar who can show how thinking is done, who can help the learner to ask and to answer his own questions and can give him practice in thinking for himself. The student must travel on his own feet.

There are some ways, therefore, in which a college or university is bad for the education of the young, and there are often better ways for the young to become educated than by attending a college—for example, by living and working in a foreign country for a year or two, or simply by working at a job for which one is responsible. Within academic institutions there is an academic atmosphere which separates the life of the mind into courses and textbooks, and requires the student to collect a specific body of knowledge. As soon as the formalities of learning descend on the student and as soon as a standard curriculum for everyone is imposed, something important is removed from the student's life. There is no longer enough variety of experience; it is all of one kind. Something happens to everything personal as soon as it is institutionalized, whether it be playing games, thinking, or loving.

The difficulty is that without educational institutions we would be forced to plan education for each child, one at a time. This was done in Europe in the seventeenth and eighteenth centuries for the members of the aristocracy and the well-to-do by a system of tutors, travel, and practical experience in society. But as soon as everyone is to have an equal chance to be educated, institutions have to be created to give it. Without such institutions we would have to find places in the laboratories of working scientists for young apprentice scientists, who would learn by sharing in one or another kind of research and would receive some kind of tutorial help from those in charge. Or it would involve working with artists and composers in their studios. Or it would involve travel to foreign countries to study the foreign languages and cultures at first hand under the guidance of native teachers. Or it would involve reading freely from suggested lists of books, with the opportunity to talk to writers, critics, scholars, and friends about the books once they had been read. It would involve practical experience in politics, in writing, and in working at a job under supervision; and it would be necessary, in a sense, to turn the whole of the older generation into one massive teaching force who would concern themselves with the young people assigned to them.

THE DEVELOPMENT OF AN IDENTITY

In the absence of such a teaching force, we assign special people to do the teaching for us. But simply because we hand over the teaching task to professionals we do not therefore need to standardize either the teaching or the learning. Teachers can, if they wish, keep the life of the student at the center of things, and think of him as a person, a person who needs a variety of practical, intellectual, social, and aesthetic experience in order to discover what there is to know and what there is about himself which he can build into a fully formed character.

The particular purpose of a college education is to enable the young to establish a personal identity from the materials of experience and knowledge which lie at hand. That experience and that knowledge do not have to be confined to the single area of the campus. At various times and in various ways, the student's experience must be enlarged beyond the campus, by including as a regular part of his education many of the things he would be doing if he were being educated by his life in the total society, without benefit of educational institutions.

It follows that, in order to achieve one's own maturity, it does not matter what specific subjects one has studied in college, or even what specific or general goal one has had there, provided that the aim is to develop as a person. What matters is that one should enjoy the work and become fully involved in it, whether the work is in science, the humanities, the arts, or technical studies. Having worked and enjoyed these studies, and having engaged in the discipline of learning during the years of college, one is then able to find ways of taking the next step, either in applying what has been learned to the practical problems of making a living and contributing something of oneself to society, or in carrying on further studies and preparation which will equip oneself for doing so.

I do not mean that the student should not see any relevance of his studies to the practical use to which they may be put, or that there should be no connection between the choice of studies and the career toward which the studies might lead. I mean that the student must allow himself to be carried along by his own enthusiasms and to follow his inclinations as to the direction his education should take.

Most of the time, educators take an opposite view of the purpose of education and deal with the problem backwards. They assume that the young must first decide, and the sooner the better, what career they will follow, or "what they will be." They must then pursue a course of study which will get them to that goal. The educators also assume that those most fitted for one career or another are those who show, through certain kinds of tests, an ability and an aptitude for learning certain kinds of subjects. The further assumption is made that unless one has these abilities and aptitudes as a child and can pass tests in these subjects, he is not qualified for education in these career subjects or in other ones.

The fact is that there are so many different reasons why children can or cannot do well in the regular school and college subjects that it is a mistake to classify their talents too specifically at any early point in their growing up. The student who does badly in mathematics or in science in his early experience with them may simply not have learned how to cope with the concepts contained in these subjects, and he may, by working in other areas of the curriculum, grow to understand concepts in general and then to understand how to deal with scientific concepts in particular. I have known students who, through the study of music and the arts in college have grown in capacity to use their intelligence in a variety of ways, and have applied that new kind of intelligence to studies which were formerly impossible for them to grasp.

In my judgment, it is also wrong to assume that everyone must have a clear-cut aim early in life and then proceed to prepare himself for a foreordained place in society. The aim of education must be to help the individual find his place among his fellow men. The first necessity is the development of one's own total character, both as a student and as a person (the two cannot, of course, be separated). For this, informal time for growth and a variety of experience are necessary. There should be no educational rushing, hounding, and harassing. Once a personal character is sufficiently well established, with its own equipment in skills and knowledge, then the question is to find ways in which a person of this ability, character, and skill can best fulfill himself in the variety of tasks which society offers. One first becomes a person, and in doing so, one finds ways of being that kind of person in action.

When the question is asked, as it constantly is, "What are you going to be?" an answer is always expected in specific terms— doctor, lawyer, corporation executive, poet. As a result, the child who grows up in America is constantly trying to answer that

question instead of the real questions of education and of what
it means to *be*. "Who am I, what can I know, what can I do,
what does life hold?" If these are not the questions which are
asked and answered, education is automatically converted into
a training program for becoming skilled in performing certain
tasks for which society rewards the performer. The ends are
static, and therefore the means become mechanical. On the
other hand, if education is conceived as the search for possibility, then the things the student does from day to day become
an integral part of that search, and the student has a chance to
find himself by the work he does; he can think of high school and
college as a way of trying himself out. If he thinks of his education in this way, he is likely to keep on trying through the rest of
his life, and he is likely to have found ways in which his life can
be fulfilled by the proper use of his talents.

Again, this is not an argument against serious commitment
of the young person to a course of action and study which
leads, for example, to a career in science, medicine, law, engineering, government, politics, the arts, or anything else. It is
to argue *for* such commitment, provided it is an honest expression of interests and enthusiasms which persist from year to
year, interests which are nourished by the inner satisfaction of
learning and developing and are unconstrained by the pressures
of premature decision and false social goals. It is also to argue
for the need to explore, to develop, to range widely, to establish new interests, to establish a self which is created around
a central core of honest preference and a clear sense of reality.

THE CHOICE OF A VOCATION

When I match my own experience in education with that of the students I have come to know over these past twenty years, I find that these ideas are confirmed in practice. I remember vividly a student who came to Sarah Lawrence College because she wanted to study music. During the years of high school she had already become a skilled pianist, and if she had been able to do exactly as she wished, she would have played the piano most of the day and composed music the rest of the time. The choice that had to be made after high school was whether to attend a conservatory of music or a college where music and the arts were taken seriously. She chose to go to Sarah Lawrence, primarily because the creative arts, including music, are central to the curriculum in the same sense as physics, literature, philosophy, or any of the other liberal arts. Since Sarah Lawrence also allows the student to choose the courses she will study and there is no standard program of studies which everyone must take, this student chose to work in her freshman year in music (composition, piano, history, and theory), psychology, and literature.

In the course in psychology, part of the work consisted in observation and study in the Sarah Lawrence Nursery School, where, naturally, this student began teaching music to the three-year-olds. As the interest in children grew and an interest in literature deepened, the student continued with the study of music, but at this point became interested in working directly in music and literature with children. She added the study of history, of philosophy, of science, and of sociology to her curriculum, yet kept as her central concern the work in music, and in her junior year composed an opera for children, involving a cast of dancers, actors, and singers, with scene designers and other friends collaborating with her in producing a work which not only delighted many audiences of children but extended the range of her knowledge into new forms of expression. She then took up the study of those technical subjects necessary to understand and practice the art of education and fulfilled the requirements for a teacher's certificate, along with her Bachelor of Arts degree. She is now a teacher of music in the public schools, the mother of three children, a pianist, and a composer of genuine talent.

But most of all, she is a person whose life has been changed and enriched by her education. In a real sense, the education was a process of finding herself and finding the best uses for a talent which, if it had been cultivated as a means simply of becoming a performing artist, might very well have ended in that particular kind of frustration which comes from developing a talent for which there is no wide opportunity for use. In the process of her education, this student learned to move directly toward the opportunities for the full expression of a self which was developing through the college work which she undertook.

One may say that the possession of the original talent in music was the reason why this student was able to find her way, and that such good fortune would not be shared by the average student—the one who does moderately well what he is asked to do, but has no outstanding ability or motivation in one direction or another.

This is partly true, but it seems to me that it is true only because educators do not seek to explore with all students the possibilities which exist within each of them. In any group of a thousand students there will be some who are better students than others, some whose gifts are more plentiful and better developed, and a large group of others who form what can always be called the average and "below-average." But this is not a reason for believing that each member of these groups cannot differentiate himself from the others by particular virtues and qualities which give him his own identity and his own way of going. Where people are concerned, it is foolish to talk of averages. There is no average except in statistics and among objects.

Among the Balinese, the children begin to dance when they are three or four years old, and the men and women of the villages dance the whole of their lives. They are not career dancers. They are fishermen, farmers, workers. The talent the children develop as dancers is not innate. Their talent develops because everyone is part of the community life in which dance is a central component, and because everyone dances. Soloists in dance and music are chosen; some of the musicians and dancers are better than others. But each person has his own place and creates a standard of performance which it is his task to raise to the utmost of its possibility. The idea that only those of exceptional talent should be recognized simply does not belong to the Balinese. They are happy to recognize special talent when they see it, but they do not consider this a reason for thinking any less of those who simply dance well, which in this case includes all of the dancers. Dancing is a part of their lives, because they grow up dancing.

I suggest that this is the way in which the arts and the sciences should be regarded in this country. It is natural to learn the arts and the sciences, and there is nothing so difficult about them that anyone but the seriously retarded cannot reach a fair level of achievement. The reason they are difficult for some children is that the arts and sciences are not a natural part of their lives as they grow up, and there are other things which are learned instead. If the development of intelligence were as central a part of the concern of American culture as the development of the dance is among the Balinese, we would consider it perfectly normal for all of our children to become proficient in the arts and sciences and to demonstrate a high level of intelligence in action.

The point is that the student, at whatever level of ability, must feel involved in his education, must be able to respond to it fully, must be able to invest himself in it. Only by such involvement will there be any possibility for individual growth or, for that matter, for developing a genuine sense of identity. The meaning of education lies in the meaning it assumes for the person who is educating himself. Otherwise there is no meaning at all, except for the artificial symbols which are used to mark those who have fulfilled the requirements of schools and colleges.

I recall another student, one who was intelligent, who had no unusual gift and no overt reason for being in college other than to become educated, whatever that might mean. Her situation would seem to me to be that of most American college students, if we allow for the usual variations in what educators refer to as average and above-average intelligence. We asked this student, along with all the other members of the sophomore class at Sarah Lawrence, for comments on the two years of education just completed, what changes there had been in her plans, what experiences had meant most to her, what seemed to her to have been the influence of the college on her life.

Her reply was, in part, "I have long since forgotten what my plans were when I first came here, except to know that they are much less ambitious now than they were then. Now I simply want to get a job when I graduate and do things for people I like."

At first glance, this might seem to be an unsatisfactory answer from a sophomore, since the end of the sophomore year is usually considered by the colleges as the time when a student should make up his mind as to what "major" he should undertake, and the first two years are traditionally considered to be the time for general education, a preliminary to making a decision about "what you are going to be."

But the answer is much better than it seems. It is honest and is part of a series of other comments of an equally direct and honest sort. The student goes on to speak of what she learned from other students at the college.

"From one acquaintance I learned that the horribly depressing characters in *Death Of A Salesman* were not meaningless and contrived, as I first imagined, but actually drawn from life. I learned that bitterness is immaturity; that it is not frightful to grow old; that when hope really ends, so does life; that we can only forget ourselves and our aloneness by concerning ourselves with others; that three-fourths of life is doing what you do not care to do, and that those who cannot accept this are truly pathetic. . . . Everything generally that you learn gives you more in common with more people and therefore gives you a better basis for knowing and understanding them. . . ."

In the case of this student, there was no dramatic development of an individual talent of the kind described in my first example. This one worked more in the field of literature than in any other during her final two years, as do many students who have not come upon the exact use of their talents and who have found in poetry, theatre, novels, essays, and philosophy a way of exploring the range of available experience. At this stage in her life, the most important contribution this student's education had made was to help her to make the connection between ideas and people, between herself and others. The truths to which she had come, about spending three-fourths of a life doing what you do not care to do, the necessity for concerning oneself

with others, the way in which an increase in knowledge means
an increase in the number of people whom you can understand
—all these had won for her the beginning of an enlightenment
about herself and her world which it is the task of education to
make possible. Once that beginning has been made, the chance
of fulfillment is enormously enhanced.

If we are talking about education as the fulfillment of possibility, there is a real question to be asked about the nature of
the process. I have said that everything depends on the quality
of the student's life, and that this must be the center of the
educational plan. How can this be arranged, and how is the
teacher involved?

THE VALUE OF GOOD TEACHING

There is a difference between a teacher and an educator, but
only in the sense that usually a teacher is thought to be one who
teaches students in a classroom, whereas an educator is one who
holds ideas about what education should be and applies them,
either in the classroom or out of it. Most teachers have ideas
about education, although many of them have expressed them
only in their day-to-day work in the classroom and have not
made them into a conscious set of ideas about education. But
the teacher who concerns himself with the life of his students
will think past the classroom and out into the total scope of the
student's experience, both on the campus and beyond it. He will
think, for example, about the opportunities the student has for
extending the discussion of the ideas of the classroom into the
general conversation of the campus. Dr. Lois Murphy, for
twenty-five years a member of the psychology faculty at Sarah
Lawrence College, held a deep concern for the lives of her
students, and went beyond the usual concern by conducting re-

search which could throw some light on the means of educational improvement available to the college.

One of the principal research discoveries of Dr. Murphy was the extent to which the living conditions of the campus and the available opportunities for free talk affected the attitude of students to each other and to themselves. Dr. Murphy writes of the way in which students are willing to try themselves out in behavior during the first year of college, behavior "which they repeat or discard after they have found out how it feels.... Others go through the trial and error experience on a verbal level, in bull sessions, or even in class—trying out ideas to hear how they sound, how it feels to voice them, and changing their ideas after they have found out which ones really make sense, or feel right. Still others go through a deeper inner process of observing, listening, moving toward a different perception of themselves and others as they go through new experiences with people, vicarious experiences in books. New perceptions leading to new behavior and feelings also arise from experience of the expectations of different people in the world of college, expectations or judgments which help them to see how things look to others, and then help them to see things differently themselves." [1]

The teacher who cares to make a difference in the lives of his students will very soon find ways in which the discussions they are bound to have with each other as they go about their campus business can be infused with ideas the teacher is presenting to his classes. He will give his students the feeling that what he is doing in class is to set some ideas and questions going which he knows the students will take further among themselves. The clear expectation on the part of the teacher that

[1] Lois B. Murphy and Esther Raushenbush (editors), *Achievement in the College Years* (New York: Harper & Bros., 1960), p. 91.

the "average" student will wish to extend in new directions is, in most cases, a sufficient motive to produce such action on the part of the student, thus setting the student free to develop his own interests and ideas.

In this way, the damaging separation of the curriculum from the extracurricular is prevented, by turning the extracurricular into an extension of the curriculum, by making the intellectual and personal interests of the classroom the center from which ideas emanate to all corners of the campus. The teacher who thinks about the life of his students, rather than merely about the subject he has been appointed to teach to them, will discover a variety of means by which their work with him can nourish their total development. The classroom meeting is merely a scheduled occasion on which the entire group of students meets together with the teacher. What he does at such meetings, and what the students know that he expects them to be doing in the intervals between the class meetings determines how far-reaching his educational influence is in their lives. If his expectation is that the students will do only as much as they are required to do, and if his conception of his duty to students is to give them the material on which they will be questioned in examinations, he will certainly receive in return the fulfillment of his expectation, but he will have little effect on their intellectual growth.

The comments of another student, one who wrote to me about her graduate work in psychology, bear upon this point. "I do not object to taking examinations nor to working very hard, but an examination is only meaningful when it is a learning experience in itself. . . . My graduate work is neither stimulating in its classes nor in its examinations, and I, who love learning, am greatly disappointed. These people care more and have more interest in and respect for the behavior of rats than of people. Their attitude is that students will not work unless they are put under pressure, that they will try to get away with whatever they can, however they can. . . . This is not education. No one is required to think, only memorize. People tell me this is the way life is, but I know it doesn't have to be, and I feel terribly sorry for those who have never known anything else and really believe this is all that's possible."

This student, as an undergraduate, did most of her work in literature and became interested in psychology and its application to human problems because of the interest in human character she had acquired through a wide range of reading. One of the most important things about her education was that it provided her with a sense of reality about what she might do and what she might become. The graduate study then became a further step toward achieving a breadth of knowledge and the practical skills necessary in the vocation to which she felt drawn, —in this case, work with disturbed children. It has also led to an interest in the problems of contemporary society, interest in philosophy, and the continuation of her interest in literature. It would have been impossible for this student to have decided, on any grounds that had meaning for her, the question of a career in social welfare until, by her education in college, she had worked through to an understanding of herself and her capacities. In coming to an understanding of herself, she also reached an understanding about her society.

Here are some of her comments, expressed in the same letter as the comments on education, about the individual in modern society. "I do indeed feel very much a child of the twentieth century—but I see a great deal that is constructive in this. I am not filled with any great New School Enthusiasm for Freud or any particular one of his followers or opponents. It may be true that all creativity is a sublimation, but I'm not at all sure that we gain anything by this knowledge. What I do feel is that people need something to believe in. In our modern world, the majority of the people seem to have rejected the idea of some all-powerful external being, often called God. They need a new place to put their faith. In other people? Yes—but that is not really possible until they have gained a sense of their own worthiness, a belief in their selves. I do not believe we are a sick society, I only feel that we are now more demanding on our individual selves than ever before. . . . I do not see the goal of therapy or analysis as being adjustment—I see it as advancement. A person who is not allowed to ask questions will not learn in any meaningful sense. In this way, he is stymied. People are stymied in many different ways at different times, but this must not necessarily preclude further growth. If you go back and reawaken the mind that has been asleep, if you stimulate, questions will arise. And if this time you see that these questions are not suppressed, but are encouraged, the individual begins to grow."

It seems to me that this student, able to think and to write in this way in the year after college, can provide us with a fair example of the meaning of education. It means to grow, to mature, to establish oneself as a person capable of creative and critical thought, able to think for oneself, and able to turn one's talent to a suitable use within the society. It also means that teachers need to be aware that students like these have nothing but contempt for those who ignore the deeper needs of the young generation and are content to dispense subject matter within the regular academic system.

The students come to college, as I did, not knowing what to expect, ready to do what is asked, ready to respond to the expectations of those whom they wish to respect and admire. What happens to them after they come is the responsibility of the educator. They can, of course, learn from each other, and they do, sometimes more than they learn from their teachers. But in the matter of intellectual and educational leadership, it is not unreasonable for them to expect more from their teachers than, at that stage, they do from themselves.

Becoming the Complete Adult
Vocationally

CHOOSING

A

VOCATION

by Elliott Dunlap Smith, Ph.D., Provost and
Falk Professor of Human Relations Emeritus,
Carnegie Institute of Technology

6

Almost everyone who earns his living devotes the greater part of his time and energies to his job. As he does this, his job and how he does it plays a large part in determining whether or not his life is happy, whether or not it brings him satisfaction, whether or not it contributes anything to others, and even what sort of a person and citizen he develops into. Your job will play this part in your life. It will do this whether you want it to or not. There is no escape. Hence, it is of great importance for you to find the right job. Doing this is called "choosing a vocation"— for the word "vocation" means "a calling," "the job you are called to do," the job which is your own particular sort of work.

Vocations can be divided into three major groups, separated from one another largely by the amount and kind of education they require.

GROUP I. *The Handwork and Clerical Vocations.* These vocations range from those of farm and industrial laborers, machine operatives, routine sales clerks, and clerical workers to those of highly skilled artisans, expert farmers, clerical experts, etc., who must have special training to qualify them for their positions. But none of these occupations requires education at the college level.

GROUP II. *The Business and Industrial Vocations.* These vocations include selling, merchandising, finance, manufacturing, and journalism. They usually call for a full college education; but except in a few specialized fields which have almost become professions, such as advanced accounting, they do not require postgraduate education, although such education is becoming more common.

GROUP III. *The Professions.* These vocations include the ministry, law, medicine, engineering, school and university teaching, research, and the newer professions such as social work, home economics, and nursing. All require professional education; and with all except engineering, secondary school teaching, and some of the newer professions, this education usually requires going to a graduate school.

Since the vocations in GROUP I are entered directly after graduation from high school, the choice of whether one of the vocations in this group is best suited to you must be made at that time. In making this choice the first question to decide is the extent to which you have the scholarly abilities and interests requisite for success in college; and then, considering your abilities and interests, and all the expense, time, and difficulty involved in going to college, whether it is worthwhile for you to go on studying or is better for you to go directly to work in a vocation in this group.

In making this decision the following points are important to bear in mind. (1) The careers in this field are the backbone of our industrial life, and are as worthy of respect as any others. (2) Today they usually enable one to earn a good livelihood for himself and his family, often more than is earned in the lower levels of success in most of the vocations in the other two groups. (3) They provide ample leisure to lead a full life and to see much of one's family and friends. (4) Almost all of

them open into the managerial vocations in GROUP II, sometimes
directly, as when a carpenter or plumber becomes a contractor,
or a farm laborer becomes a farm manager; and sometimes with
the aid of night-school or other part-time study. Hence, if you
later develop managerial capacities and interests, having entered
a vocation in GROUP I will not have deprived you of the chance
to get into managerial positions. (5) The vocations in GROUP I
involve no more drudgery than the lower levels of work in the
other vocational groups. (6) Most high schools have vocational
counselors who can help you decide whether you are really
suited for higher education, and if not, which of the vocations in
this group you are most likely to succeed in and to enjoy, and
what special training, if any, is desirable.

Since this chapter is focussed upon the two vocational groups
which require higher education, from now on it will be assumed
that the reader has decided to go to college or is now in college,
and is considering entering one of the vocations in GROUP II or
GROUP III.

PART I—THE NATURE OF A VOCATION

How do you choose a vocation wisely so that you will always
be glad of your choice? A good way to start is to find out what
it is in a vocation that will enable you to find happiness in it;
that will enable you to use it to become the sort of person you
want to become; and that will enable you to do something with
your life that, as you look back upon it, will give you satisfaction
with what you have accomplished. Let us examine these questions one by one.

*1. What is it in a vocation which will enable you to find hap-
piness in it?*

In pondering this question, most young people start by think-

ing of earnings and wonder in which vocation they will earn
most. The answer is this: With a few exceptions, the difference
between bottom earnings and top earnings in any one of the
vocations in GROUPS II and III is so much greater than the difference between different vocations in earnings at the same level
that, with a few exceptions, the vocation where you will earn
most is the vocation in which you will do best because it is most
suited to your abilities and interests.

Moreover the differences in earning opportunity between vocations vary from time to time, and what is today a vocation with
a high demand for men and exceptional opportunities both to
earn and to get ahead, in a few years may be overcrowded, slow
in promotion, and low in pay. Salary differentials are thus a
changeable thing; but in choosing a vocation you are choosing a
life's work and should look to enduring values.

Another thing which young people are quick to think about
when considering whether they will find happiness in a particular vocation is the amount of drudgery which it will involve.
What, then, about drudgery? Every vocation demands work, and
hard work and routine work are part of getting ahead in all of
them. But drudgery is a different thing. What is drudgery for one
person is not drudgery for another.

With drudgery, as with earnings, the difference between the
several vocations is small compared to the enormous difference
between the "drudgery" involved in doing your daily work if
you are in a vocation in which you are interested and for which
you are fitted, and the drudgery involved if you are in one which
neither arouses your interest nor fits your abilities. If you are
fitted for a vocation in ability, you will soon learn to do its
routine work swiftly, with little effort, and it will cease to be
distasteful. If your vocation enlists your vigorous interest, tasks
that would otherwise be dull and even distasteful will be vital-

ized. For example, think of the drill and hard routine that the athletes on your varsity teams and the musicians in your college orchestra and chorus go through gladly, and then think of what drudgery doing this same drill would be to someone who has little athletic or musical ability or interest. For drudgery begins only when the burdens and distastefulness of work are so great, and the sense of accomplishment and interest in work are so small, that as you work what you are doing no longer seems worthwhile.[1]

Interest in work begins with doing things you care about. What you care about may be artistic expression, it may be efficient organization, it may be doing well in competition, it may be curing physical or mental ills, or leading men to a better way of life or to higher knowledge and skills—it is different with different people—but interest and happiness come when the things you accomplish through your work are things *you* deeply care about. Unless this is so and your vocation is suited to you in this respect as well as in ability, joy in accomplishment will be lacking and your work will be pleasureless. Moreover, if you have interest in any particular sort of work and enough determination to struggle to attain excellence in it, the absence at the start even of some important qualification is not fatal. Just think of what Helen Keller has done and the happiness she has found in her work in spite of her tremendous handicaps.

Finally, high among the things which bring happiness in a vocation is the fellowship of co-workers—of men you enjoy working with and get to know through work as you can in no other way. But this fellowship best arises between people who work well at the same job and care about the same things in their work, and this means between men who in capacities and

[1] See R. C. Cabot, *What Men Live By,* Chapter 1, "Work, Play and Drudgery," for an excellent discussion of this problem.

interests fit the job they are doing. If a man doesn't fit his job and is a bungler, or if he cares little about what he is working at, he will be a burden to his colleagues and an outsider from the fellowship of their working team. Any of you who have been on an athletic team, or in a musical or dramatic production, for instance, know this. In a lifelong vocation it is even more true.

Happiness on the job, then, comes from many things. In very large measure it comes from earning an adequate living; from the joy of doing work which is suited to you and which calls for your best; from the joy of getting results and doing service which you value; and from the fellowship of co-workers.

No one vocation in itself provides these sources of happiness much better than another. In each of these ways, what will enable your vocation to give you happiness throughout your working life and contentment as you look back on your life's work after you retire, is its fitness to your abilities and interests, and your fitness to its demands and its satisfactions.

2. What in a vocation will cause it to help you become the sort of a person you want to be as, day by day, what you do on your job and how you do it casts its steady influence upon you?

In the first place, as with happiness, your vocation will do little to develop you unless it provides work which you can put your heart into both because its standards and ideals are those you share and because you care about the results you strive to get. If your work violates your ideals, it will debase you. If you work listlessly and without purpose, you will dry up and shrivel. Look around you at the middle-aged persons whose hearts are not in their work and see. Moreover, if your vocation is to lift you out of a self-centered, unhappy round and develop you, it must provide work which in some measure you care about because of the service it renders to others or to society.

In the second place, if your vocation is going to help you develop it must provide work which asks for the best that is in you, and then, as this work develops you, leads to harder tasks, greater responsibility and the freedom to accept this responsibility. This means again that it must provide work for which you are fitted and care about.

In the third place, if your vocation is to develop you, it must provide a never ending opportunity to learn. For if you stop learning, you stop developing and begin to decline. In intellect and character, human beings are like trees. If they stop growing, they tend to decay. The chances—indeed, the necessity—of learning from study and from experience in all the professions in GROUP III are almost endless. In the business and managerial vocations of GROUP II there is relatively less chance to learn from study, but wide chance to learn from experience. In both groups the chance to learn is greater if a person has ability and driving interest, and especially if this ability and interest cause him to move steadily ahead to higher levels with the new environment and new problems that such promotion brings. Here again, it is fitness for your vocation that matters.

Finally, to help you develop your vocation must cause you to work with colleagues who, because they share your interests and ideals, enlist your respect and affection, and thus influence you from day to day toward becoming the sort of person you want to be.

3. What will enable a vocation to provide opportunities for you to give the sort of service which you want to give and which will bring you lifelong satisfaction?

The different vocations vary greatly in the opportunities to render service which they provide. Each gives its special chance to serve. The opportunities to be of service afforded by such professions as the ministry, teaching, politics, medicine, nursing, or social work are far more clearly apparent and more direct than those afforded by law, engineering, journalism, merchandising, or manufacturing. But it is easy to overemphasize this. For these latter professions also provide, though in less conspicuous ways, values essential to civilized life. In addition, in their human contacts they provide endless inconspicuous opportunities for important service to individuals, and in the position which they give one in the community they provide significant opportunities to be of public service.

Fully as important as the opportunities which your vocation provides are your capacity to discover them, your eagerness to seize them, and your ability to use them well, all of which depend upon fitness and interest. A teacher or minister who is not suited to his vocation and has little interest in it, for example, gives little that is of value. An able and perceptive foreman, who cares about those who are under him, may not only give significant service to them by providing leadership and order in their work, but may find himself close enough to their lives to do as much for their development as their teachers or their ministers do. Again, a public-spirited, able manufacturer, whose fitness for his vocation has enabled him to rise to a position of distinction in his company and his community, quite apart from the service he renders through the development of his company and its products in the regular course of his job, may do more for the development of his community than any of its politicians or public servants.

The happiness which you will find in your work, its influence upon your development, and the quality of the service which your work will give, are thus all primarily dependent upon how fully you are fitted to the demands of your profession and how fully in its ideals and satisfactions it is fitted to you.

In considering your fitness to various vocations, it is important to recognize that cutting across these vocations are fundamental functions, such as selling, managing, research, or teaching; and it is these vocational functions, as much as the individual vocations in which they are performed, which will determine the abilities required and the satisfactions provided by your work. Some vocations, such as the wholesale selling of merchandise or schoolteaching, involve but one function. Others involve several. For example, merchandising usually involves selling and administering as well as buying; and university teaching involves research as well as teaching. Moreover, most professions have branches, each emphasizing different functions. In manufacturing, for instance, there are positions emphasizing technical research, sales, merchandising, financing, and personnel functions, as well as administrative functions. Again, in a single profession, such as engineering, medicine, or law, there are research, design, and teaching functions, as well as the function of the practitioner. Moreover, in addition to these functional divisions all of the professions have special fields, such as surgery, pediatrics, and ophthalmology in medicine, or the business, insurance, real estate and tax specialities in law, each with its functional divisions and its special requirements and satisfactions.

Thus, not only may the different aspects of a single vocation be suited to people of widely differing abilities and interests, but a young man has considerable opportunity to find his way to the work best suited to him after he has entered upon his vocational career. Yet in spite of these variations within the vocations and these opportunities for feeling one's way, there are such large differences between vocations in respect to the abilities which they require and the interests which they satisfy, that the choice of a vocation suited to your abilities and interests is of vital significance to your happiness, to your development, and to the service you will be able to render.

PART II—THE PROCESS OF WISE VOCATIONAL CHOICE

How then can you best find out what vocation is best for you?

First: It is desirable to start thinking systematically about what vocation is best for you as soon as you get under way in college. This will give you time before a final decision has to be made to reach tentative decisions, to explore and test them, and then to change them or confirm them in the light of what time and experience has taught you.

Second: It is important to get clear on three things you should not consider lest they muddy your thinking and bias your decision. These things are:

1. For the reasons we have discussed before, do not be influenced in your choice of a career because you think there is a greater demand for men or a chance of higher earnings in one vocation as against another. You are courting disaster if you seek to speculate on the job or salary markets.
2. Do not be influenced in your choice of a vocation by the fact that you have been offered, or think you can get, some particular job. In the long run no job in a type of work for which you are unsuited will prove a good job for you. Only after you have chosen your vocation and are faced with the immediate problem of deciding what companies to apply to for a job, should either the relative chances of getting a job or the relative opportunities which available jobs provide for progress in your career influence your decisions.

3. Do not be influenced in your choice of a vocation by what you think will please your parents. Give thoughtful consideration to their reasons. Then make up your own mind as to which vocation you are best fitted for in ability and interest. Few things which you can do will bring greater unhappiness to your parents than to enter a profession for which you are not suited in order to please them, and then expose them over the years to witnessing the limited success and the distress which being in the wrong profession has caused you.

Third: It is important to clear your mental decks for action by getting firmly in mind that the only thing you are trying to do is to find what your true abilities and enduring interests are, and then find to what vocation they are best fitted, so that as you repeat certain sorts of tasks year after year and get certain sorts of results in pursuing your vocation, you will do your work well, will rise in your chosen field, will get pleasure from what you do and contentment from the results you obtain, and finally will be helped by your work to develop into the sort of person you want to become. For this is the heart of your problem.

Fourth: In choosing your vocation it is important to follow a well-ordered plan. To suggest what such a plan might be, I have prepared the two plans which follow.[2] Neither is better than the other, and you may design a plan that is better for you than either of these. The important thing is to have a carefully thought out plan that is suited to you, and to follow it. At first it may be best to feel your way by following your chosen plan very informally, making first one tentative decision and

[2] The substance of these plans was first outlined by the author in "Choosing a Career," *Mechanical Engineering,* January, 1946, pp. 27-32.

then another; but as you near the point of final decision, I think
it will pay to follow formally and explicitly each of the steps outlined in the plan you have chosen.

PLAN I

1. Think over and make a list of the vocations you might possibly want to enter and for which you think you might be
qualified.

Don't divide vocations too narrowly. Stick to the major vocations, and do not narrow your consideration down to specialized fields until your choice of a major vocation is firm.

2. Cross off, one by one, those vocations that, as you consider
them more fully, are definitely out until you have reduced your
list to the two or three that seem best.

Do not hurry, but keep at it and keep thinking and exploring
until you have reduced your field of choice to two or three possibilities. Until you do this, you are in no position to make the
thorough study of the vocations you are considering which is
essential to a wise choice.

3. Find out all you can about what the two or three vocations
which you have selected require and what they provide, asking
yourself and answering such questions as these:

A. In each of your selected vocations what sort of things
will you be doing day after day and year after year? What
will be your principal tasks? What subordinate things must
you do to accomplish them? For example, if you have selected
selling as one of your alternative vocations do not assume that
the obvious work of calling on customers and presenting your
product to them is all that selling involves. Instead, ask yourself such questions as: Must I travel extensively? Will much
of my work consist in figuring or clerical routine? Must I

analyze mechanical or other problems? Must I constantly take risks because I am paid on commission?

Be especially careful to find out what sort of routine work you will have to do. There are routines in every vocation—sales routines, research routines, care-of-patient routines, parish routines, teaching routines, and so on. Such routine work is a substantial part of every vocation, and the routine of the vocation you select will play a vital part in making the vocation you choose good or bad for you.

B. What will the environment of your work be? Where will you work? What sort of people will you be among, and what will your relationship to them be? How will it affect your home life, etc.?

C. What does the work lead up to, and how will it change as you grow older and progress? What are the requirements for progressing?

D. What opportunities to learn does it provide, and what freedom to change does it give?

It may not be easy for you to find the answers to these questions, but it is important to do so. Good books on what people do in the various careers, even biographies that are frank and reliable, are rare; but they are worth searching for. Trade journals may help. The best source of information, however, is asking people in the fields you are interested in just what they do day after day, what it takes to do it well, what they like and dislike about their work, *and why*.

You will be wise to ask persons of different ages so as to get an over-all picture. It is especially important to ask persons who are between five and ten years older than you are, since they have had enough experience to know the facts and are young enough to see the problem from your point of view, as older men cannot. To get information in this way you must keep at it; but if you have persistence, somehow you can get at the facts, and in the process of finding them out for yourself, you will get a fullness of understanding that no one person or book can give you.

To help you explore the professions which you are considering, I have appended to this chapter "Notes on the Principal Vocational Functions," which outline the qualities that the functions demand and the satisfactions they afford.

4. After you know what the two or three careers which you have selected will demand and provide, ask yourself how well you are suited to each.

A. Think over the principal qualities it is important for you to have in order to succeed in doing well each part of the work of each vocation under consideration, and how fully you possess those qualities.

B. Examine your past experience and see if you can find instances which indicate whether or not you were right in each estimate of your abilities. Get down to "brass tacks" on this. For example, if success in a career which you are considering involves much analysis of documents, think of the most difficult reading you have done as a basis for solving a problem, what difficulties it involved, how successful you were, and why.

C. In the same way, think out concretely for each tentative career: the interests it will satisfy; the particular sources of discontent, of happiness, of self-development, and of service that it will provide; and just what these will mean to you at the start and over the years. Here again, look at concrete instances, seeking for evidence against as well as for your initial conclusions. Be sure to pay attention to the routine aspects of your work and how acceptable or distasteful they will be to you. They will play a large part in your happiness on the job.

For example, if you are considering teaching chemistry in college as a career, and know that success will involve devotion to research, think over the time you have spent in the laboratory. How far did getting your measurements painstakingly exact excite you and make you want to stick at it? How much satisfaction and sense of accomplishment did it give you to repeat an experiment and get a result somewhat more precise than before?

Remember, it is exceedingly easy to fool yourself about both your interests and your abilities. Don't jump to conclusions. Go carefully over your work and extracurricular activities for *specific evidence*. Then when, on the basis of concrete evidence, you think you have or lack certain qualities or interests, look for evidence on the other side.

D. Compare the suitability to your abilities, interests, and personality as thus determined of the few careers you have examined and decide which one is your first choice. In doing this remember that your abilities, personality, and interests are not fixed, but are subject to development, and consider how much you can develop those in which you are deficient. But be very careful not to fool yourself on how much you can change.

E. Work up what you have thought out into a brief, clear statement which gives both your conclusions and the main evidence in support of them. When you have done this you can forget your career for a while and still not lose the value of what you have done.

PLAN II

For many persons it may be better to reverse the order of this analysis and pursue the following plan:

1. Think over the things you have done and what they indicate about your abilities and about your interest, that is, the type of work results and work environment that give you satisfaction.

2. Put your conclusions on these points down in a *well-organized, well-written outline*. This plan requires writing from the very start if it is to get anywhere. For when one is analyzing himself, it is my experience that writing as one goes is the only way to keep one's thinking from becoming sloppy, wishful, and self-deceiving.

3. Check each conclusion on your outline by a careful review of the evidence which your past experience gives as to its validity and make annotations and changes accordingly. (See 4B and C in PLAN I.)

4. Make a list of all the vocations you might want to enter and for which you might be qualified. (See 1 in PLAN I.)

5. Cross out, one by one, those vocations that are definitely out, until you have reduced your active list to two or three possibilities. (See 2 in PLAN I.)

6. Find out all you can about what the few vocations you have selected require and provide. (See 3 in PLAN I.)

7. Compare your conclusions about your abilities and interests with what is required and provided by the two or three alternative vocations you have narrowed down to, and reach a decision as to which one of them is best suited to your abilities, personality, and interests.

8. Write down your final conclusions and the evidence in support of them in a compact outline.

In carrying out your plan, don't lean too heavily on others. Think everything out for yourself before getting advice. Even after getting advice, make up your own mind. You cannot delegate to others, even experts or parents, your responsibility for your own competency or for making your own major vocational decisions.

It is true that there are some psychological tests of aptitude and of interest which, if you are seriously perplexed, might give you help provided they are skillfully given and cautiously interpreted, but first complete your analysis to the best of your ability. Then if you are still so puzzled that you feel tests are needed, keep away from the people who claim that they can tell you once for all what you are best suited for. Instead get a good doctor, university professor, or college guidance bureau to recommend a reliable test psychologist and go to him. Remember that even then you will have to use your own judgment as to what is best for you, since no test can give you more than a few indications to balance with others in making up your own mind.

PART III—TESTING YOUR CHOICE OF A VOCATION

Once you have completed a careful analysis according to your chosen plan, forget your career for a while. Then some weeks or months later go at it again. Review what you have done and see how well it stands up. Then test out, in your college and extracurricular work, the abilities and interests you thought you had to see if they are what you thought they were. College can give you a fairly good preview of what you can do and what you will enjoy doing in your vocation. Moreover, if you test out your choice of vocation in this way, you can do much to strengthen the qualities and interests you need for it. You will get more out of your education if you know the aims, interests, and demands of your life work. You will choose your vocation better if you test out your fitness for it by seeking to make what you do in college, as well as in professional school, a means of making you more fit for and interested in the career which you have chosen as your vocation.

In doing this don't overemphasize the specialized knowledge, techniques, or interests related to your vocation. Remember that more important than all else are the broad, fundamental qualities and interests that relate to success and happiness in your chosen field, and that these will increase in importance as time passes and especially as you work up in your field. Also, the development of these general qualities will give you greater freedom of choice in making vocational decisions as you move forward in your career.

If in college you explore through reflection, experience and testing out in your college work what your true vocation is, you will form valuable habits which will go on after you are at work; you will equip yourself to take advantage of the many vocational choices that come, and to discover chances to choose which otherwise would be hidden; and, above all, you will be finding your way step by step to a life work for which you are fitted and which will increasingly extend and develop your powers to rise and to serve—a life work, which calls for the best that is in you and which satisfies your deepest needs and desires.

APPENDIX—NOTES
ON THE PRINCIPAL VOCATIONAL FUNCTIONS

These NOTES deal only with broad vocational functions, not with specific vocations. Since, as has been said, individual vocations often combine two or more of these functions, and frequently permit a choice between two or more alternative functions, it is necessary, in considering a vocation, to get clearly in mind what vocational functions it involves.

In order to be brief, these NOTES provide no particulars about the qualifications and satisfactions which they list; nor do they discuss how the same qualification or satisfaction differs in different vocations. They do not mention, for instance, how different in each instance is the intellectual excellence so important in all research, when the research is in medicine, in the exact sciences, in law, or in the humanities. Hence, to know what the various points listed here will mean in reality when you enter your chosen vocation, you must find out in as full and intimate detail as possible what the work of each vocation you are considering actually is, and thereby bring the broad terms of the NOTES to life. Also, since the points are suggestive and not comprehensive, it is important with each point to look for qualifications and satisfactions not listed therein. Reading these NOTES or any other printed statements about vocations does not diminish the importance of exploring your intended vocation with people who are in it, finding out just what they do, what they like from day to day, and what gives them satisfaction and develops them from year to year. The following points below can help you see what to look for as you do this, but to get anything of value out of them you must do the looking.

The Scholarly or Artistic Functions

RESEARCH demands, above all else, outstanding and highly educated intellectual ability in the particular field in which the research is done. It also demands an interest in the subject of the research sufficient to prevent the exhausting, meticulous, often discouraging work necessary for the precision and thoroughness that lead to discovery, from becoming drudgery. It further demands exceptional perseverance. Its greatest satisfactions lie in the enjoyment of doing scholarly work, in the excitement of intellectual attainment, and in the chance of sharing in the development of one's field.

DESIGN. *Technical design* is similar to research in its qualifications and satisfactions. It requires greater resourcefulness and inventiveness than research and less scholarly excellence. *Artistic design,* such as in architecture, requires artistic creativeness as well as technical competence.

ARTISTIC AND LITERARY PRODUCTION at the top levels, whether in music, art, drama, or literature, requires not only great talent but creative genius. It also demands such drive toward creative excellence that the artist or author will be willing to go to any length in practice and self-discipline, and in years of hardship and struggle without recognition, in order to perfect his creative powers. Even if he succeeds in attaining high stature, he may not have outstanding recognition during his lifetime. His greatest satisfaction, therefore, must often come solely from his devotion of his life to his ideals.

Once an artist, composer, or author drops below the highest level, the requirements of genius, dedication, and perseverance drop. But in order to find employment, he usually must subordinate his art in considerable measure to the requirements of the institution or publication where he finds employment; and as a performer, writer, or teacher, he will have to do much that is repetitive and often routine. But he will have the great satisfaction that will come from working in the field of the art or literature that he loves.

The Professional Functions

TEACHING, in any field, demands an interest in young people and in what is being taught which is sufficient to enable the teacher to go over the same subject at the same level year after year; struggle with the same difficulties of the same pupils day after day; provide and supervise the drill necessary for the acquisition of skill; read and correct countless papers; and yet, in the thrill of seeing his pupils learn his subject and develop as persons, find all these tasks satisfying, and not tedious.

At the more advanced scholarly levels, teaching demands less interest in young people and greater interest and ability in the subject being taught. At the university level, it merges with research, and becomes an equal part of a research scholar's vocation, with the demands and satisfactions listed above.

But at every level it requires the strength of character and force of personality to order classroom behavior; the imagination and colorfulness to hold interest; and the poise, character, self-restraint, and sympathy sufficient to enlist the confidence of students and exercise leadership over them.

While, relative to other professions, especially at top levels, its financial rewards are low, it has long vacations and other compensations, and it provides the deep satisfaction of having played a part in developing the minds and character of those whom one has taught.

THE PROFESSIONAL PRACTITIONER, whether in law, medicine, the ministry, architecture, or the newer fields such as personnel or public relations, must combine competent knowledge and

skill in his field with the common sense and breadth of understanding of the personal, social, economic, or other aspects of
his client's problems, so as to be able to go beyond his particular
field and decide what should be done, considering his client's
problem as a whole. Hence he must have intellectual ability and
interest, a broad education, an interest in people, the qualities
of mind and character which make people trust him, the mod-
esty, insight and strength of character which will enable him to
influence them, and the integrity to make that influence valid.

His work is likely to be highly demanding. His greatest satisfactions consist in filling a position, which, if he is successful,
brings status, early responsibility and self-reliance, and above all
involves the doing of skilled work of direct value to others.

The ministry demands of the minister the qualifications of the
teacher as well as those of the practitioner. More than in other
professions, a clear and deep sense of "calling" supported by
courage and integrity is vital. Few vocations have as deep satisfactions if one has adequate dedication and capacity to meet its
temptations and its difficult demands; and few are so devastated
by shallowness of mind, lack of integrity, or feebleness of
dedication.

The Industrial and Business Functions

SELLING, in any field, calls for the capacity to combine pleas-
antness with shrewdness and persuasiveness in dealing with
people. A salesman must have the type of personality which enjoys the reiterated, superficial contacts with sales prospects
which are inherent in getting close enough to people to sell to
them when the time is ripe. He must also be willing, in considerable measure, to subordinate his social and personal life to
his work. But in his work he is his own master to an unusual
extent, his salary is more directly responsive to his own efforts

than in other functions, and if he enjoys competition, he has the satisfaction of doing directly competitive work. In certain fields, such as real estate, the salesman is also a trader.

TRADING, whether in goods, in securities, or in real estate, calls for a high degree of commercial shrewdness, a capacity to survey an economic situation, discovering and appraising slight clues which others miss, and the ability to take large speculative risks without undue nervous strain. The trader must be able to work long hours under tension. His chances of making large financial gains, and also losses, are exceptionally high.

BUYING AND MERCHANDISING call essentially for insight as to what will appeal to customers and shrewdness in dealing with those who make or sell it. The buyer or merchandiser, while usually on a salary and more of an organization man, thus needs many of the qualifications and receives many of the satisfactions of the salesman and trader. But he also needs something of the creative interest in his product of the designer. In large industrial concerns merchandising may directly involve trading, and in small stores, etc. may be combined with selling.

ADMINISTRATION AND MANAGEMENT, whether in industry, stores, banks, or institutions, is a broad and highly varied function. At the lower levels, it may be essentially the supervision of technical or clerical routine, where the qualifications demanded are primarily technical or clerical competence, an interest in order sufficient to sap routine of its dullness, and a capacity for precision, thoroughness, and supervision. On the other hand, management at these levels may be predominantly the management of men under conditions where a competent knowledge of process and product (usually learned on the job) must unite with the perceptive interest in others and the warmth, force, and integrity of character needed to become a leader. The satisfactions of this sort of manager, in addition to those of attaining efficiency of operation, may include the gratification of developing the men he leads.

At the higher levels, the demands of administration broaden until the administrator must combine the qualifications of salesman, merchandiser, and even trader with those of a manager, including the capacity to sense in advance the character and ability of the men to whom he delegates responsibility. Even more than a practitioner, a true administrator must be able to deal with problems as a whole, taking account of all that might affect his decisions. To do so, he must have a broad education and the alertness and breadth of mind to deal with branches of the business in which he has had neither instruction nor experience, learning from others, often from subordinates, often from specialists, and often from his own mistakes. Finally, he must have the capacity to make decisions on broad problems with patient awareness of the importance of precision and of significant detail, and of the necessity for those at the top often to work longer hours under greater strain than those under them.

With most industrial functions, at any but the routine levels, a large part of the satisfaction consists in the development of efficiency and the excitement of competition similar to that provided in sport.

*Becoming the Complete Adult
Politically*

THE YOUNG CITIZEN
IN A
WORLD LIKE THIS

by Harry A. Overstreet, Ph.D., Professor Emeritus of Philosophy and Psychology of the College of the City of New York

and

Bonaro Overstreet, author and lecturer in Adult Education

7

THE psychologically healthy citizen is one who identifies himself with many sectors of life: family, school, occupation, neighborhood, church, community, the world. In each of these he participates with interest and a feeling of belonging. In each of them he has a stake and therefore a status. Each is a kind of "home base" for him. He draws strength from it and lends his strength to it.

The psychologically unhealthy citizen, on the other hand, is one who identifies himself with hardly any sectors of life. For such an individual even home may become little more than a place, in Robert Frost's words, "where, when you have to go there, they have to take you in."

Psychologically speaking, the secret of citizen strength is identification-with, while the most dangerous source of citizen weakness is alienation-from.

When, therefore, we think of a psychologically sound citizen, we think of one who has a sense of "belonging" in the major spheres of life: domestic, educational, recreational, religious, economic, and political.

If we were to select one sphere in which identification is not so likely to be as immediate and vital as in the others, we would doubtless select the political or citizen sector. This would probably not have been true in the years of town-meeting government. Then participation was part of the job of living and of working with one's neighbors. The town meeting was, as it were, a neighborhood home. Here adults met together in common council, identifying themselves with concerns shared by all. Nowadays, except in small rural and village areas, this comfortable at-homeness with neighborhood concerns has largely disappeared. Memories of it, and some of the habits of it, may linger among the older generation (the very much older); but among the younger generation no such memories or habits exist. Born into a metropolitan and international age, they know politics mostly as something distant and episodic. Among many persons, and particularly among young persons of today's wide-flung world, the political or citizen relationship is least intimate of all.

This condition of citizen alienation is one of our present democratic anxieties. If government of and for and by the people calls for identification as wide as a people's concerns, how can it be sound and vigorous where the identification is almost wholly with non-citizen, near-at-hand concerns—of home, business, play, etc.? How can it be wisely and productively focussed where voting is largely neglected, candidates are scarcely known, and issues hardly understood. In such a situation, citizenship becomes reduced almost to a nullity.

At a time like this, when democracy is seriously threatened, the question whether citizen-quality is sound or unsound becomes of central importance.

MASS PRESSURISM

Where there is little or no citizen identification among young people, we find that three dangers tend to manifest themselves. One is the simple ignoring of the political sector: indifference. The second is the constant derogation of what is done in that sector: cynicism. The third is the substitution of mass pressure for intelligent identification: pressurism.

Confining ourselves for the moment to the third, there is a growing tendency around the world today among young people to substitute for the sound democratic process of open-minded dissent the demagogic process of mass-action. Mass-action, as now increasingly practiced, seems to have certain characteristics that are not only destructive of the democratic process itself but antithetical to individual citizen-maturing. For one thing, such mass-pressuring among young people tends to be almost wholly negative and generalized, so that it directs the attention of the young citizen away from, rather than toward, the detailed practical problems that have to be solved. In the second place, and most disturbingly, such mass-pressuring among young people rewards conformity with the crowd and penalizes individuality of judgment, even though such groups of young citizens characteristically hail the right of individual dissent as a cause they are defending. In the excitement of mass-pressuring, they do not encourage dissent except as unanimous, that is, as engaged in by the entire group against the ongoing operations of a constituted government. This looks dangerously like the forming of mass-mind.

Obviously, such conformity-in-dissent, with the pressures put on each individual neither to look at problems in their precise detail nor to exercise his own judgment, is far removed from the kind of dissent the protection of which has been the achievement of democratic institutions. Hence, we might say, the young citizen requires first and foremost in his citizen life identification with that process of individual freedom of thought which is unique in the democratic experiment.*

AMERICAN POLITICAL TRADITION

The first prerequisite of competent American citizenship, we would say, is a warm and intelligent identification with the American tradition. This tradition still lives in the great documents of our history: the Federalist Papers; Declaration of Independence; American Constitution; Jefferson's writings; Lincoln's addresses; and so on. One of the manifest shortcomings of our American approach to citizen preparation in our country that is perhaps partly responsible for the lack of intelligent interest in political issues is that we relegate the reading of these robust and revealing documents to the school years, when minds are still too immature to grasp their full significance. Such reading in the schools is, of course, admirable and essential; but the more effective reading and study should be done in the adult years. It is too easily forgotten that these documents were written by adults, discussed by adults, fought for by adults. They are, in short, *adult material*. And very mature spiritual convictions undergird such political expressions, especially those pertaining to human rights, the protection of human integrity and freedom, and the indefeasible equality of all men by virtue of their Creator. We must rightly count it a grave omission, therefore, that in our organized adult education programs—as like-

* It is to be noted with some concern that a Marxist journal, *New Horizons for Youth,* has recently been launched in the United States under Communist editorship. This journal will undoubtedly do its utmost to encourage among American young people the demoralizing practice of mass-pressuring.

wise in college and university courses—little, if any, intensive study is made of these vital American documents. Thus the young adult is given small chance to move into intellectual and emotional closeness to the great intentions of the country in which he is to play his citizen part.

This is of particular significance at the present time when the social, political, and moral stature of our country is under review throughout the world. The citizen of today must of necessity inform and fortify his mind with the compelling arguments that led to an experiment unmatched in history.

This will require a rethinking of the kind of education that the young citizen should have. After recalling the deep roots of our tradition of justice under law that go back to the Magna Charta, one young American lawyer of distinction has made a suggestion that we would hope might sometime be widely adopted. "I should like," he writes, "to see every college and university add to its curriculum an undergraduate course in 'Principles of Anglo-Saxon Justice.' [We would further the suggestion by making it apply to every program of adult education.] The object of the course would be to make available to every student . . . the fundamental principles of our legal and judicial system and to suggest the tone and climate of our legal rules of fair play. I would try to give our . . . students a 'feel' for the meaning of basic rights, for the right way and the wrong way of judging evidence, of sifting truth from untruth, of measuring liability or guilt, of making up one's mind. Such a course could, with broad strokes, trace the need of law in society and the forces and rules which have shaped and nourished our legal system. I would try to impart a true understanding of those things which are the flesh and bones of our pattern of justice— freedom of speech, of religion, of press; the right to be secure in our homes against unreasonable searches and seizures; the right to a jury trial in all criminal prosecutions; the right to counsel; the right of habeas corpus; the guarantee against double jeopardy, self-incrimination, ex post facto laws, and bills of attainder; and the right of due process of law.

". . . In short, I believe there is a place—a vital place—in our structure of liberal education today for the exposure of all students to the time-tested principles of justice so that as many as possible may understand how rights are granted or acquired, how justice is administered, and what makes law and order secure in a republic." [1]

We quote this at some length because of its basic significance to the citizen-function. These are the essentials of justice in any country that aims to make the rights of the individual the center of its concern. They find no place in regimes, like those of totalitarianism, that make the individual the tool of the state or of a ruling "party" in the state.

PRINCIPLES OF POLITICAL FREEDOM

In line with the above suggestion of a basic course-in-training, we would ourselves suggest two others. The first is "The Principles of a Free and Responsible Government." We are aware today of dangerous lapses of knowledge in this area. We find such lapses disturbingly displayed—"writ large," as it were— where formerly unfree societies make their difficult advances into freedom. Government of and for and by the people gets curiously distorted into government of and for and by the ruling group. Perhaps the most signal weakness has been the inability to realize the indispensability to all free and responsible govern-

[1] Sol M. Linowitz, "Law, Freedom and Liberal Education," *The Journal of the American Association of Collegiate Registrars and Admissions Officers,* Vol. 33, No. 1 (October, 1955), p. 33.

ment of an uncoerced and unharassed "loyal opposition." Coercion and/or harassment of the "opposition" has taken various forms, from imprisonment of dissenters to confiscation of property and of opposition newspapers. Even in our own relatively seasoned democracy, government in power has not been averse, in its own interest, to withhold undesirable factual information from the public.

Another principle of political freedom with which the citizen will need to identify is what we might call "Diversity in Unity." This is what uniquely marked our own break with the traditional systems of government and our advance to a new political theory and practice. All the older forms of government had characteristically operated from the top down and from the center to the periphery. The emphasis had been on unity as directive of the diversity. The American Revolution, starting with the assumption that all men are created equal, saw in government the instrumentality through which men could themselves, in spite of their diversity, create their own government and keep it free. The emphasis was and still is on the diversity that generates unity.

This is emphasized in the highly perceptive book by the French Dominican monk R. L. Bruckberger, *The Image of America:* [2]

The founders of the American Republic believed that the best way to safeguard the common good and national unity was to entrust them as far as possible to the private initiative of free individuals. In this they were truly original. They were convinced that no political system in the history of the world had relied enough on the resources, the intelligence, and the

[2] R. L. Bruckberger, *The Image of America* (New York: Viking Press, 1959), p. 106.

good will of the individual. They knew the risk this involved, and a terrible civil war was to justify their fear. Yet they considered even the risk of civil war less dangerous to the common good of Americans and to national unity than any curtailment of freedom, and that is why they insisted upon the right to rebellion as an essential part of their political concept. They have been proved right.

Then he adds: "All the administrative controls and all the despotisms together cannot build so united, so powerful a nation as liberty." In fact, he anticipates what such diversity-in-unity would mean for the European nations: "I feel certain that if the day comes when the European nations, instead of moving toward more and more centralizing, move toward more and more individual autonomy and give private initiative the greatest possible scope, Europe will once again astound the world."

PRINCIPLES OF A FREE ECONOMY

In this "citizen-training" curriculum, we would suggest also a third course: "The Principles of a Free Economy."' The major conflicts throughout the world today have come to a burning focus in an outright challenge to a free economy. The American citizen will need to be equipped with as clear an understanding as is possible of what is involved in such an economy.

From the point of view of what seems to have worked best in our own developing economy, the following would appear to be its essential requirements:

In the first place, it must be decentralized. "Decentralization means that we have millions of centers of initiative instead of one," as Henry C. Wallich says in his book *The Cost of Freedom.*

In the second place, in order to have the greatest possible flexibility, initiative, and responsiveness to people's needs, it must be a "market" economy, neither completely state-owned nor completely state-controlled. In the third place, it must be competitive. "Competition," to use Wallich's words, "stimulates each to do his utmost." Nor need competition mean, as many have been led to think, "the devil take the hindmost," or "winning by fair means or foul." Part of the vigor of our free economy comes from the stimulus that resides in doing one's best in order to do what is better than what has been or is being done.

In the fourth place, we seem to have discovered that a free and responsible economy must develop what John Kenneth Galbraith has aptly called "countervailing powers." Neither management nor government must be permitted to tyrannize over the worker; nor the worker, in combination, over management or government. The voluntary balancing of powers over against one another would seem to be an essential of every free and responsible economy.

Again, a free and responsible economy, even though highly competitive, will permit and encourage voluntary co-operation all across the board. Such co-operation amid competitors, we find in the multitude of national, state, and regional associations formed among competitors in the economy. Every large city is constantly staging one or another meeting where competitors sit in friendly conference and talk over their common problems. We remember, with some amusement, the utter disbelief of a visitor from the Near East who sat with us at a dinner of the American Booksellers Association. He simply could not understand how competitors could sit in friendly conference and even display to one another their competing wares. He felt there must be something phony about the meeting: either it was make-believe or the government was secretly in control.

Finally, as we have learned through the rugged necessities of our system, a free economy must have its adequate *agencies of compassion*. The unemployed worker, for example, must not be thrown ruthlessly on the dust heap: unemployment insurance must be available to him. Nor must the individual who has suffered an industrial accident be left unhelped, nor the person who, because of his age, is retired from his job. All of this kind of dependable, institutionalized help is new in the world. It infuses the system with a spirit of compassionate obligation that underscores the worth of the individual.

PARTICIPATION IN CITIZENSHIP

But the plot now thickens: courses of study such as we have suggested will not alone create wise and responsible citizens. Lenin knew this. "Without labor, and without struggle," he wrote in *What and How to Learn*, "book knowledge about communism is absolutely worthless . . . In every village, in every city, the young should actually perform some task of social labor, be it ever so small, be it ever so simple." John Dewey knew it, and said it briefly: "Learn by doing." Psychologists now tend to reduce it to a single word: "Participate."

Speaking of how not to educate for citizenship, Gordon Allport writes: "No amount of verbal defining will convey the meaning of such concepts as 'his Majesty's loyal opposition' or 'fair play.' To most Germans, loyalty is identified with obedience." [3] In fact, as we have ourselves discovered, political re-education in West Germany is largely conceived of as listening to lectures.

In our own history as a people, the practice of citizenship has

[3] Gordon Allport, *Personality and Social Encounter* (Boston: Beacon Press, 1960), p. 186.

been developed chiefly through voluntary associations. On the pioneering edge, it was mainly by getting together for neighbor help; in village communities, it was by way of the town meeting; in the Revolutionary War, it took the form of Committees of Correspondence. In our current society, it takes the form of numberless voluntary associations: political parties; citizens' planning groups; community welfare associations; parent-teacher associations; chambers of commerce; help-giving organizations; community drives; and many others.

No person, we would say, has taken the necessary steps to a dynamic citizenship unless he has learned to be a participant in a number of such social, economic, and political associations. This, in our country, has been the main road to citizen "identification."

By the time he is eighteen years old, the youth can join a number of organizations that bring him into active relations with community needs: church groups, recreational groups, study groups, community service groups, civic improvement groups. In each of these he will be not only taking part in an activity but weighing values that will become part of his personality structure for life. By the time he reaches voting age, practically all community associations are open to him. He need be, then, no longer an outsider, as he so largely was in his childhood and early adolescence. He can now be a "member" and begin to perform what Lenin called "his task of social labor."

Such participation is now possible on an even wider scale. The Peace Corps is a project that has been designed to enlist young Americans in working relationships within the underdeveloped countries of the world. Many are concerned with a "select corps of exceptional college graduates" for this work; but one distinguished educationalist of labor, Victor G. Reuther, pointedly insists that the usefulness of the Peace Corps must not be limited entirely to youth with university training. In fact, he argues for the greater need in these underdeveloped countries for "young men and women who have skills in the mechanic arts, in the building trades, in metal working, in the repair and maintenance of machinery and communications equipment"—capacities acquired by experience in our technically oriented culture—and who can be of use where technical experience is now almost wholly lacking.

Whatever form the Corps may take as it continues to develop, it embodies the vision of a new, wide-flung method of participation in the social, political, and economic upbuilding of emerging peoples. Through such participation, our youth may well be helped to become, in a very real sense, "citizens of the world."

FREEDOM FOR NEW COUNTRIES

The young adult of today lives in a time of unprecedented concern. On the one hand, underdeveloped countries, in numbers never known before, are making their impatient advance into freedom. On the other hand, powerful countries strive for the obliteration of hitherto achieved freedoms. In the one case our sympathies, in the other, our fears, are aroused. The young citizen will require the best intelligence, on the one hand, to respond to the hopes for freedom and, on the other, to cope with the threats to freedom.

We speak currently of the hopes for freedom as "revolutions of rising expectations." The term is a revealing one: it marks a point of new demand among the underdeveloped peoples of the world. It may even—if it succeeds—mark the beginning of a new achievement in world advance. In short, it is quite possible that if these revolutions succeed, we shall witness "a new birth of freedom" throughout the world.

Robert Frost reminds us that we started it all. We made a declaration of independence that the world has not forgotten. Speaking of those revolutionary Americans, he writes, in "Dedication": [4]

> So much they knew as consecrated seers
> They must have seen ahead what now appears,
> They would bring empires down about our ears
> And by the example of our Declaration
> Make everybody want to be a nation.

So these are *our* revolutions.

But there are lions in the way. One of them is the sheer unpreparedness of the revolutionary peoples for the tasks ahead of them. The freedom which looked wonderful from the viewpoint of unfreedom can look distressingly different when the freedom to resist unfreedom has been changed into the freedom to make freedom work.

One attitude which the more fortunate countries could take might be that of letting the newly emerging peoples master their own difficulties. This might, indeed, have been possible in simpler times of the world. But when relatively inexperienced peoples attempt nowadays to make their advance into a highly complex system of technological, economic, and political arrangements, the willingness to let them learn by doing it themselves may not be the most happy solution of the problem.

So the obligation rests upon the more fortunate peoples of the world to be of help; and it at once becomes apparent that the help must be more than physical. Our own good fortune lies

---

[4] From "For John F. Kennedy His Inauguration," a much longer poem from *In the Clearing,* by Robert Frost. © 1962 by Robert Frost. Reprinted by permission of Holt Rinehart & Winston, Inc.

in the fact that we had time to advance from the crude operations of an agricultural economy to the highly refined and complex operations of an electronic economy. Also, we had time to make the gradual changes in human arrangements called for by such a new economy.

While we must, then, offer physical aid, our deeper and more essential offerings must be psychological and spiritual. We who have learned must help these others to learn. But this is a highly difficult thing to do. Our own learning has been accomplished not only by slow steps covering almost two centuries but within the framework of a Western culture. These others live within totally different environments of history and culture. The processes and end results of our own growth cannot, therefore, be automatically transferred to the peoples of these other cultures.

This is the Number One problem that confronts all who would help these newly emerging peoples to make their way soundly into a new freedom. The problem is indeed a novel one, and few in our culture have as yet been trained to comprehend it in such a way as to meet its demands. Even our political scientists are aware that they themselves, for all their scientific training, know far less than enough. In their book *The Politics of Developing Peoples,* Gabriel Almond and James Coleman say: "... the disciplines of political science until recent years have been working in a limited sector of man's experiences with politics—the modern, complex, primarily Western states." In short, our political scientists find that they have a far too restricted knowledge of human associations to provide reliable guidance in these newly emerging lands.

Here, then, is new territory for the young citizen of this generation. He must learn what his forefathers never had the need to learn: how to know people of alien cultures well enough —their history, customs, needs, and prides—so that he can join in building an attitude and a method of help that will really help.

A second problem with regard to these emerging peoples is far more serious. It is the problem of color. In spite of a Civil War that aimed to solve it and in spite of governmental efforts in the present years, that problem is still with us in our own land. It takes virulent form in South Africa, where *Apartheid* is a shameful cruelty. It rears its head even in the homeland of the Magna Charta, where the cry is heard: "Keep Britain white!" And even in Soviet Russia, where loud profession is made of racial tolerance, shocking reports come of mistreatment, in the Soviet "Friendship" Universities, of the invited African students.

Color may become the most embarrassing and frustrating problem of the coming generation of citizens. In attacking this deeply controversial issue, the young American citizen who, in mind and spirit, rightly belongs to a new generation will not hesitate. Born into a proud tradition that has held not only Magna Charta but the Declaration of Independence and the Emancipation Proclamation, he will want, above all, to get on with the new, pressing task of extending freedom in the world. Whether the opposition to the extension of such freedom goes by the name of white superiority, or racial purity, or *Apartheid,* or Jim Crow, he will have none of it. Time is rapidly running out for this long and cruel form of injustice of man to fellow man; and the young citizen may well have the good fortune, in his lifetime, to see the end of it. In any event, disciplined as he has been to fair play and compassion, he will have his clear job of freedom-making cut out for him.

In this area of "rising expectations," far the easiest problem to solve—and yet itself difficult enough—will be that of assigning the requisite aid, in loans and grants, to help the newly developing countries to make their break-through into the modern world. This will require little more than good will and an intelligent sense of needs. But even here, we have not yet acquired the know-how; and the citizen of the new generation will be the first in a long line of learners.

THE CHALLENGE TODAY

The toughest problem the young citizen will face—indeed all American citizens, young or old—should not be difficult to identify. For over forty years now, this problem has been growing more critical; and it bids fair to be with us for years to come. From Woodrow Wilson on, our leaders have been hard put to it to know how to deal with Communist strategy, for it has been something new under the sun. It has not been, as in traditional diplomacy, a strategy of negotiable adjustments, but a strategy of utter and determined irreconcilability. Now this strategy has mounted to a crisis point, threatening the very survival of ourselves as a people and as a way of life.

It has taken us a long time to realize the precise nature of this problem. Even now, Americans of good intentions, but still dangerously ignorant of the facts, innocently believe that if we would only be nicer to the Communists—less belligerent—peace on earth would be achieved. The time for such naïveté is long since past; and the citizen of the new generation will accept it as one of his primary obligations to be knowledgeable about the facts. We of the older generation can at best pass on our own experiences of misunderstanding and hope for better seeing.

The problem has now reached its third stage. First came Lenin; then Stalin; now there are Khrushchev and Mao. Khrushchev is perhaps the most dangerous of the four, because he comes "bearing gifts." What these gifts of "peace and friendship" really mean will be for the citizen of the free world to discover. If, as everything in past strategy, from Lenin on, would seem to show, these "gifts" merely mean a breathing space when non-military pressures will be substituted for military pressures, the citizen of the free world will not be taken in. He will remember that the basic purpose still remains unchanged.

The young citizen of today has one signal advantage over his elders: the record of Communist tactics and intentions is far clearer than it was when leaders like Churchill, Roosevelt, and the others were forced to try to comprehend its baffling maneuvers. Churchill called communism "a riddle wrapped in a mystery inside an enigma." To those who know their way around in today's world, it is no one of these: it is a plain intention spoken in double talk that most of us now begin to understand.

It is little wonder that our past leaders made grave mistakes about this strange new entrant into the world. Their mistakes are pardonable, even though a hundred million people in the satellite countries now live in social, economic, and political enslavement who might today be free if the mistakes had not been made. The really unpardonable thing, however, would be for the present generation, with the record now clearly at their command, to make similar or worse mistakes.

This record of communism's doings—its endless breaking of promises; its takeover of peoples through infiltration and deception; its suppression of freedom among its own people and its expressed intention of doing likewise throughout the world—all of this has brought us to a new era in world history.

Also, we are quicker now to understand Communist "code" language. When Khrushchev says, as he did not long ago in a big meeting in Moscow, "We have helped and shall go on helping people fighting for their freedom," we now know clearly what he means: namely, that Communists will go on stirring up every organized Communist minority in the world—anywhere and everywhere—to overthrow the constituted government. And when he says that they will go on "helping people" into their "freedom," we know what this means: namely, that these Communist minorities—hard-core revolutionaries—will terrorize people into submission.

All of this means that the new generation should be able to see with new eyes and act with clearer intentions. Thus the considered words of President Eisenhower's nine-man committee delivered to him on the eve of his retirement are justified: "We are now in a period when the mission and style of diplomacy are changing. . . . The prospect is for a period of protracted non-military conflict between the Free World and the Communist system" which "will reach into every portion of the globe."

New approaches will be needed in our major relationships throughout the world. For these new approaches, new knowledge will be of the essence. But also there will be required a new kind of dedication. We cannot in these days—whether we are young or old—afford the quietude of isolation or of indifference.

In a time like this, when the very life of freedom is critically at stake, the best words, perhaps, for the toughening of the spirit are those of Lincoln, spoken on the battlefield of Gettysburg: "that we here highly resolve . . . that government of the people, by the people, and for the people shall not perish from the earth."

Lincoln spoke to an older generation. President Kennedy spoke to a younger generation when, in his inaugural address, he said:

> The world is very different now. For man holds in his mortal hands the power to abolish all forms of human poverty and all forms of human life. And yet the same revolutionary

beliefs for which our forebears fought are still at issue around the globe—the belief that the rights of man come, not from the generosity of the state, but from the hand of God.

We dare not forget today that we are the heirs of that first revolution. Let the word go forth from this time and place, to friend and foe alike, that the torch has been passed to a new generation of Americans—born in this century, tempered by war, disciplined by a hard and bitter peace, proud of our ancient heritage, and unwilling to witness or permit the slow undoing of those human rights to which this Nation has always been committed and to which we are committed today at home and around the world.

Let every nation know, whether it wishes us well or ill, that we shall pay any price, bear any burden, meet any hardship, support any friend, oppose any foe to assure the survival and success of liberty.

This much we pledge. . . .

As a new generation takes up these extended obligations, it may well find that a new concept of man's social, political and economic relationships is developing. Already the physical spaces have been made to vanish. It may yet turn out that the most furious and irrational of man's mental and emotional antagonisms may be made to vanish. Already a new idea begins to possess the fragmented world: that sovereignty can be maintained by community gained. Men are struggling with this idea in Western Europe (Benelux, the European Coal and Steel Community, Euratom, the European Common Market, etc.); and in the Atlantic area, through the difficult stages of the North Atlantic Treaty Organization. More dimly, and yet with some persistence, men are struggling in this direction in Asia, Africa, and Latin America. In short, a world-wide type of "communities" is in the making; and world-wide concepts of administration and law begin to take shape.

The young adult will inevitably become part of these wider movements of social, political, and economic integration. And the time may not be too far distant when, involved thus in the totality of mankind, he will add a new dimension to his civic responsibilities and count himself a citizen of the world.